—Diseases and People—

PARKINSON'S DISEASE

Alvin and Virginia Silverstein
and
Laura Silverstein Nunn

Enslow Publishers, Inc.

40 Industrial Road	PO Box 38
Box 398	Aldershot
Berkeley Heights, NJ 07922	Hants GU12 6BP
USA	UK

http://www.enslow.com

Library of Congress Cataloging-in-Publication Data

Silverstein, Alvin.
    Parkinson's disease / Alvin and Virginia Silverstein and Laura Silverstein Nunn.
       p. ; cm.—(Diseases and people)
    Includes bibliographical references and index.
    ISBN 0-7660-1593-9
    1. Parkinson's disease-Juvenile literature. [1. Parkinson's disease.
    2. Diseases.]
    [DNLM: 1. Parkinson Disease-Popular Works. WL 359 S587p 2001] I.
    Silverstein, Virginia B. II. Nunn, Laura Silverstein. III. Title. IV.
    Series.
    RC382 .S56 2001
    616.8'33—dc21
                          00-012073

Printed in the United States of America

10 9 8 7 6 5 4 3 2

To Our Readers: We have done our best to make sure all Internet addresses in this book were active and appropriate when we went to press. However, the author and the publisher have no control over and assume no liability for the material available on those Internet sites or on other Web sites they may link to. Any comments or suggestions can be sent by e-mail to comments@enslow.com or to the address on the back cover.

Illustration Credits: Agricultural Research Service, photo by Ken Hammond, p. 56; AP Photo/Julie Jacobson, p. 92; AP Photo/Marty Lederhandler, p. 6; AP Photo/PA, p. 98; AP Photo/PPL Therapeutics, p. 99; AP Photo/Tim Shaffer, p. 89; © Corel Corporation, p. 105, © Sinauer Associates, Inc., p. 40; Cover of *Awakenings* VHS tape, p. 47; Department of Neurosurgery, University of Florida, courtesy of David Pearce, p. 78; Dover Publications, Inc., p. 17; Harold Wade, pp. 33, 34; National Cancer Institute, p. 51; National Institute of Neurological Disorders and Stroke, pp. 10, 12, 65, 67; National Library of Medicine, pp. 14, 15, 19, 23, 25, 46, 62 (both); Reproduced from the collections of the Library of Congress, p. 49; Thanks to David Sulzer, Depts. of Neurology and Psychiatry, Columbia University, p. 22; United States Office of Personnel Management, p. 28.

Cover Illustration: AP Photo/Marty Lederhandler

Contents

PARKINSON'S DISEASE

What is it? A chronic, progressive disease of the nervous system in which nerve cells in areas of the brain responsible for controlling body movements, which secrete a messenger chemical called dopamine, die off.

Who gets it? Mainly middle-aged and elderly people, but it can also strike young adults (young-onset Parkinson's). It occurs all over the world, and in both men and women (slightly more often in men).

How do you get it? A small percentage of cases are hereditary, but in most cases there is no known cause. Suspected causes include environmental pollutants.

What are the symptoms? Tremors (shaking), muscle rigidity (stiffness), impairment of balance and coordination, and slowness of movements. Dementia, swallowing difficulties, speech problems, and other secondary symptoms occur in a minority of patients.

How is it treated? Drugs that replace the lacking dopamine (e.g., levodopa), substitute for it (dopamine agonists), or prolong its action in the brain (entacapone, deprenyl) are used singly or in combination. Surgery destroying small amounts of brain tissue (pallidotomy, thalamotomy) and deep brain stimulation with electric current may relieve symptoms. Transplants of dopamine-producing nerve cells into the brain are being used experimentally.

How can it be prevented? Because the cause is unknown in most cases, there are no reliable methods of prevention. Antioxidants have been suggested.

Actor Michael J. Fox rose to fame with his starring role in "Family Ties." In 1998, he announced that he had been diagnosed with Parkinson's disease seven years earlier.

The Shaking Disease

Canadian-born actor Michael J. Fox has had a long career in TV and movies since he first arrived in the United States at the age of eighteen. He got his big break in 1982, when he won the role of Alex P. Keaton on the television show, "Family Ties." Fox was twenty-one at the time, but he was able to play a teenager because of his young, boyish appearance. During the show's seven-year run, Fox won three Emmy Awards and a Golden Globe for his role. On the set of "Family Ties," he met Tracy Pollen, who became his wife in 1988. They later had four children: Sam, twins Schuller and Aquinnah, and Esme.[1]

Michael J. Fox is also well known for his role in the successful Back to the Future movie and its sequels. He has also starred in a number of other movies over the years. In 1996, he returned to TV in a new series, "Spin City," in which he played a deputy mayor. "Spin City" was another success, and Fox won three Golden Globes for his role. His life seemed picture-perfect, but

Fox was keeping a personal tragedy hidden from the public. In 1998, he announced that he had been living with Parkinson's disease for seven years. This is a disease that usually affects people older than fifty—and Michael J. Fox was only thirty at the time of diagnosis. "I love the irony," says Fox. "I'm perceived as being really young, and yet I have the clinical condition of an old man."[2]

Fox first noticed symptoms in 1991 when he was on the set of the movie *Doc Hollywood* in Gainesville, Florida. Fox had felt a strange twitching feeling in his left pinky finger. He went to a local hospital where a neurologist (a doctor who specializes in the nervous system) told him that he probably did something to his funny bone. Within six months, however, the twitching had spread to much of his left hand and his shoulder was stiff and achy. Once he got back to New York City, Fox went to another neurologist and underwent a variety of tests. He was shocked to find out that he had Parkinson's disease. Fox says that he kept his condition hidden from the public because it was something he wanted to handle in private with his family and some close friends. His doctor told him that he would be able to function normally for many more years, but the symptoms started to worsen over the next few years. Fox started to get severe tremors (involuntary trembling or quivering) and stiffness in his entire left arm. Then, he developed a constant stiffness in his hips, tremors in one or both hands, and a "tapping feeling" in his feet. Sometimes his arms and wrists became so stiff that he could not even pick up the TV remote control.

Michael J. Fox takes medication to control his symptoms, but it takes time for the drugs to take effect. On the night of the 1998 Golden Globe Awards, Fox's left arm and leg were shaking so badly that he could not even get out of the limousine until the drugs kicked in. He was in no condition to greet the reporters and photographers, so he told the driver to drive around for a little while. "He probably thought I was nuts," he said about the limousine driver, but Fox wanted to wait until the symptoms were under control before he made his appearance.[3]

Fox elected to undergo brain surgery to alleviate the severe tremors in his hand that could not be helped by medication. The surgery was successful, but he continues to use medication to control the remaining symptoms.

How did Michael J. Fox manage to hide his condition for so many years? He says it was possible through increasing amounts of medication, through surgery, and by using "a billion tricks I can do to hide the symptoms," such as moving around or touching something to briefly stop the tremors.[4]

Fox decided to go public with his condition in 1998 because he wanted to help other people with Parkinson's. He decided to quit "Spin City" so that he could devote his time and energy to his family and to finding a cure for Parkinson's disease.[5]

Michael J. Fox has had a major impact in the fight against Parkinson's and has greatly increased public awareness about this debilitating disease. In 1999, he testified before Congress, urging a $75 million increase in funding for Parkinson's research. (In 1997, Congress had approved $100 million to be used for Parkinson's research.)[6] He has set up the Michael J. Fox Foundation for Parkinson's Research, and has created a Web site for anyone who wants to help the cause.[7]

Michael J. Fox remains optimistic about his prognosis. At age thirty-eight, Fox told *TV Guide*, "I'm completely confident that in my fifties this will be gone."[8]

Michael J. Fox testified before Congress in 1999, hoping to gain an increase in funding for Parkinson's research.

Before the 1960s, people with Parkinson's disease did not have much in the way of treatment. They could expect to end up in a wheelchair three to five years after the first symptoms appeared. Now, however, Parkinson's disease is no longer considered a hopeless condition. Scientists have developed effective medications that can help most patients control their symptoms and live manageable lives. It is now common to live at least fifteen or more functional years after diagnosis.

Parkinson's disease is not a single disease. The name is used to describe a number of conditions that exhibit similar symptoms. The main symptoms include tremors (shaking), muscle rigidity (stiffness), poor balance, and slowness of movements. Scientists often refer to conditions that involve these kinds of symptoms as parkinsonism. Parkinson's disease (PD) is the most common form of parkinsonism. PD has no known cause, but other types of parkinsonism may involve a variety of causes.

Parkinson's disease is a disease of the central nervous system that worsens gradually over time. Patients typically experience uncontrollable shaking and muscle stiffening. As the disease progresses, symptoms become more severe, until some patients can no longer walk, talk, or take care of themselves.

In Parkinson's, the neurons (nerve cells) in special areas of the brain become damaged and eventually die. These neurons are responsible for controlling body movements. They normally work by sending messages through other nerve cells and ultimately to muscle cells, causing them to contract. Chemicals called neurotransmitters help in carrying messages from one nerve cell to another. Most of the nerve cells in the area affected by PD use a particular neurotransmitter called dopamine. When key nerve cells are damaged, the dopamine production in these areas of the brain drops. As a result, the nerve messages cannot be sent effectively. When enough nerve cells are lost, symptoms develop.

Researchers are working hard to find out what causes Parkinson's disease. Meanwhile, they have developed treatments that can help control the symptoms. For example, the discovery of dopamine's role in Parkinson's has led to the creation of medications that replace the missing dopamine and, therefore, can reestablish communication between nerve cells. Knowledge of the precise areas of the brain that are affected by PD has allowed the development of surgery to help patients whose symptoms are not relieved well enough by drugs. In the controversial procedure of fetal tissue transplants, the patient's lost nerve cells are replaced with dopamine-producing tissue from fetuses.

Health experts recommend that the best way for Parkinson's patients and their families to cope is to learn as much as possible about the disease and what treatments are available. In addition to drug therapy, exercise and diet are an important part of managing the disease. Although it is not yet possible to stop the disease from progressing, these techniques can allow patients to live more productive lives.

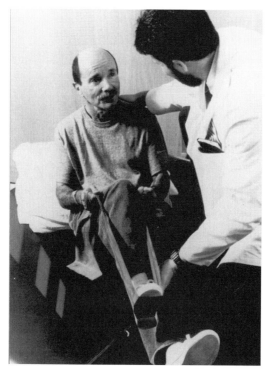

Doctors encourage Parkinson's patients to exercise their muscles. Exercising can help improve balance and enhance body strength so that the patient is less disabled.

2

The History of
Parkinson's Disease

English physician James Parkinson published a paper in 1817 called "An Essay on the Shaking Palsy." This was the first detailed description of the disease that was later named after him—Parkinson's disease. James Parkinson came to his discovery quite by accident. He became intrigued when a colleague told him about an interesting yet mysterious case. A fifty-year-old gardener was having problems doing his work because of a trembling he felt in his left hand and arm. The patient had no idea what might have caused this kind of shaking feeling.

The patient's symptoms sparked Parkinson's curiosity. He decided to study people in the London streets in hopes of spotting victims with shaking palsy, or *paralysis agitans*.

As Parkinson walked around town, he spoke or a sixty-two-year-old man, who had had the disease for about eight or ten years. This man walked with great difficulty, had a stooped-over

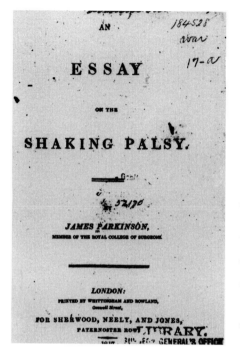

In 1817, James Parkinson published the first detailed description of the disease that would later be named after him.

posture, and had speech problems. He told Parkinson that his condition had developed gradually.

Another man, who looked impressively athletic at the age of sixty-five, had such a severe stooped posture that he could move only by running instead of walking, leaning heavily on his cane.

Parkinson studied one man from a distance. This man could walk only by having a helper in front of him, supporting him with a hand on each shoulder while the man rocked back and forth. In this way, he built up enough momentum to run. Then it was a race for about twenty paces, until he ran out of energy and the helper caught him to keep him from falling on his face.

Parkinson's landmark paper on shaking palsy included just six cases, and only one of them was actually his own patient. Parkinson admitted that his study was incomplete and the descriptions were based on pure speculation and comparison. But his explanations were, for the most part, close to the present-day descriptions of the disease. In "An Essay on the Shaking Palsy,"

Parkinson described the condition: "Involuntary tremulous motion, with lessened muscular power, in parts not in action and even when supported; with a propensity to bend the trunk forward, and to pass from a walking to running pace: the senses and intellects being uninjured."

Parkinson also went on to explain that the symptoms typically start out as a tremor (an involuntary shaking or quivering), which comes and goes in one limb, usually in the hand, arm, or head. The tremor gradually worsens and becomes uncontrollable. Eventually new symptoms develop, such as stooped posture, fatigue, and walking difficulties. He also mentioned problems in controlling the muscles. In addition, Parkinson made a distinction between shaking palsy and the tremors seen in other conditions such as epilepsy, or tremors associated with drinking too much tea, coffee, or alcohol.[1]

Parkinson's work did not get much recognition until the mid-1800s. After reading Parkinson's essay, a French physician and teacher, Jean-Martin Charcot, decided to do further

In 1876, physician Jean-Martin Charcot suggested that the disease be called "Parkinson's disease."

research into shaking palsy. Charcot improved Parkinson's original description by adding muscle rigidity to the list of symptoms. In 1876, Charcot described a patient who showed signs of rigidity, but no tremors or paralysis. As a result, he rejected the name *shaking palsy* and suggested that the disease be referred to as Parkinson's disease in the future, in honor of James Parkinson.[2]

Tremors Through the Ages

Although Parkinson's disease was first described only two centuries ago, scientists believe that this disease may have been around for thousands of years. After studying ancient records describing tremors and other symptoms, many modern scientists believe that these patients may have had signs of PD.

Some of the earliest evidence of Parkinson-like symptoms has been found in Sanskrit texts dating back to 2500 B.C. An Egyptian papyrus dated 1350 B.C. also described PD symptoms.[3] In the second century A.D., Greek physician Galen of Pergamum, who made important medical discoveries and developed many modern research methods, wrote about different kinds of tremors. He distinguished between a resting tremor, one that occurs at rest, and an action tremor, one that occurs during movement. Galen may have been describing symptoms of PD, but he did not relate the tremor to any other symptoms.[4]

During the late 1400s, Italian artist Leonardo da Vinci wrote about "human beings who tremble without permission of the soul," which some historians believe could have been a description of PD.[5]

A famous etching by seventeenth-century Dutch artist Rembrandt, "The Good Samaritan," shows an innkeeper with a stooped-over posture holding out his hands with his thumbs touching the forefingers. PD patients often make this movement, known as "pill rolling." Over a century later, German poet Johann Wolfgang von Goethe noted that the innkeeper appeared to have tremors in his hands.[6]

Also in the seventeenth century, German physician Franciscus Sylvius de la Boë confirmed Galen's description of two kinds of tremors. Sylvius reported on tremors

In the late 1400s, Leonardo da Vinci (whose self-portrait is shown here) wrote about "human beings who tremble without permission of the soul."

that occurred during an activity such as writing or walking and those that exist while the body was at rest. He noted that the resting tremor was much more common than the action tremor.[7]

In the mid-1700s, German physician Johann Juncker also distinguished between two kinds of tremors: active and passive. He believed that active tremors were brought on by strong emotions, such as fear and anger. Passive tremors had a physical basis, such as aging and palsy.

Around the same time, Francois Boissier de Sauvages also studied tremors and made further observations. He observed that trembling limbs continued to vibrate even when supported, and could be temporarily stopped by voluntary movement. He also noted that some patients would walk quickly or run just to keep their balance.[8]

When Parkinson published his work on the shaking palsy in 1817, he incorporated not only his own observations but also many of these historical accounts of tremors and accompanying symptoms in patients. Parkinson, however, was the first person to point out that they were all parts of a common condition.[9]

Searching for Answers

Jean-Martin Charcot was responsible for making Parkinson's a well-known disease. In 1861, Charcot and a colleague, E. F. Vulpian, wrote a series of articles on Parkinson's disease, which helped to increase public awareness of the condition.[10]

By the late 1800s, scientists had gained a better understanding of most of the brain structures and their functions. Italian anatomist Camillo Golgi developed a stain that made it possible to examine the neuron's anatomy. Golgi showed that the brain was made up of billions of individual microscopic nerve cells called neurons. Each consisted of a cell body, containing a nucleus and other internal structures, and numerous tiny, thread-like branches. Golgi's discovery allowed scientists to gain a better understanding of how the brain works. Medical experts used this knowledge to learn more about Parkinson's.[11]

In 1895, Professor Édouard Brissaud believed that the problem causing Parkinson's might lie in the *substantial nigra*, a cluster of black-pigmented nerve cells found in the basal ganglia, an area deep within the brain. However, autopsies at that time were not conclusive. Brissaud could not determine whether the damage was due to disease or simply due to aging.

In 1912, Frederick H. Lewy studied autopsies of some Parkinson's patients and found tiny abnormal spherical structures in some brain cells. These days, most medical experts consider these "Lewy bodies" to be an indication of Parkinson's disease. Lewy bodies are found in about 75 percent of cases.

In 1919, a medical student named C. Tretiakoff confirmed Brissaud's findings of the substantial nigra's role in Parkinson's. In

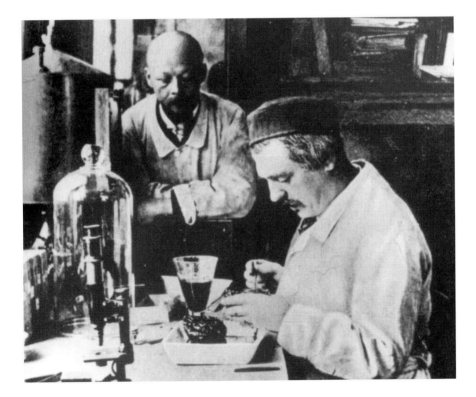

Professor Édouard Brissaud believed that the problem causing Parkinson's might lie in the substantial nigra.

twelve autopsies of Parkinson's patients, Tretiakoff discovered a definite abnormality: He found damaged cells in the substantial nigra, with a loss of pigmentation. But Tretiakoff could not figure out why this caused patients to have tremors, a stooped posture, and stiff muscles.[12]

In 1938, German pathologist Rolf Hassler did extensive autopsy research on the substantial nigra in Parkinson's patients. His work confirmed Tretiakoff's findings, showing evidence of damaged nerve cells in the substantial nigra. But Hassler's work went unnoticed because it was during World War II, when people were more concerned about injured soldiers.[13]

Scientists came up with conflicting theories on the significance of the substantial nigra in the brains of Parkinson's patients. British physiologist Sir John C. Eccles suggested that electric currents crossed from one nerve cell to another. German pharmacologist Otto Loewi and British physiologist-pharmacologist Henry Dale, on the other hand, believed that chemicals called neurotransmitters carried messages between nerve cells.[14]

By the 1950s, new technology made it possible for scientists to observe and measure neurotransmitters. A group of Swedish researchers, led by Arvid Carlsson, used a staining technique more advanced than the one Golgi had developed to view the substantial nigra, the corpus striatum, and other key parts of the brain. The researchers discovered that these areas normally have large amounts of dopamine, a chemical that is produced in the substantial nigra and carries messages to the corpus striatum, which controls movement, balance, and walking.[15]

A Key Chemical

In Vienna, medical researcher Oleh Hornykiewicz read about the Swedish researchers' work and came up with the idea that a lack of dopamine might be the cause of Parkinson's symptoms. In an autopsy, he studied the brain of a Parkinson's patient and found this was indeed the case: There was practically no dopamine in the striatum. Hornykiewicz teamed up with Viennese physician Walter Birkmayer, who was studying Parkinson's disease. They showed that the dopamine-producing cells in the substantial nigra of patients with Parkinson's disease are damaged, and the dopamine levels drop. As a result, the striatum does not receive enough dopamine to control body movements. Hornykiewicz suggested a way to replace this dopamine deficiency.

In 1960, Hornykiewicz and Birkmayer treated Parkinson's patients with levodopa, or L-dopa. L-dopa is a chemical that the body can convert to dopamine. Although dopamine itself cannot cross from the general bloodstream into the brain, L-dopa can. Unfortunately, they had trouble finding the right dose to use. The improvement of the patients' Parkinson's symptoms was only temporary. When the researchers tried increasing the dose, the patients developed serious side effects, including severe nausea, vomiting, and low blood pressure. The doctors were discouraged by the results. Although they published their studies in 1961, L-dopa was not used as a practical treatment.

Six years later, American physician George Cotzias did further experiments with L-dopa in the hope of eliminating the severe side effects that occurred in the patients treated by Hornykiewicz and Birkmayer. Cotzias discovered that L-dopa caused nausea in patients not because it reacted badly with the digestive tract, but because it affected a small area in the brain called the vomit

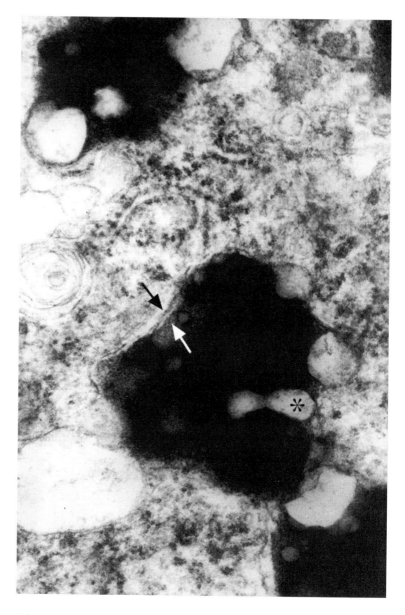

This image of Lewy bodies in the human substantia nigra is magnified 190,000 times.

center. Cotzias studied the effects of L-dopa on seventeen patients. First, he gave them a low dose of L-dopa—too low to bother the vomit center. Then, he very gradually increased the dosage until it was even stronger than the doses given by Hornykiewicz and Birkmayer. The results were quite different: Some patients still suffered from nausea, faintness, and occasional vomiting, but since the doses were increased only slightly each time, the vomit center was able to get used to the presence of L-dopa, and the side effects gradually disappeared. Cotzias's studies showed that L-dopa improved both rigidity and tremors. This was an exciting development for Parkinson's patients.

Physician George C. Cotzias studied the effects of L-dopa and found that it improved both rigidity and tremors in Parkinson's patients.

In the May 27, 1968 issue of *Journal of the American Medical Association*, Dr. Cotzias reported impressive results with L-dopa treatment in twenty-six patients. After hearing about Cotzias' success with L-dopa, other doctors did further studies on L-dopa to confirm Cotzias' findings. In 1970, the Food and Drug Administration (FDA) approved levodopa and it soon became the standard treatment for Parkinson's disease.[16]

Today, levodopa is used in combination with other drugs to increase the chances of effectiveness. In addition, a variety of other drugs are available to help control Parkinson's symptoms. Brain surgery is also an option for patients whose severe symptoms cannot be helped by medications.

On the Cutting Edge

Doctors have been experimenting with the use of brain surgery to control Parkinson's symptoms since the late 1930s. In 1939, Dr. Russell Meyers made an interesting discovery while performing an operation to remove a brain tumor. He found that by making a cut into the corpus striatum, he was able to relieve his patient's tremor and rigidity. Dr. Meyers then repeated the procedure with other patients and noticed that their symptoms improved, as well. He noted that the best results occurred when he made a cut deep into a cluster of nerve cells in the basal ganglia. This bundle of nerve cells connects the corpus striatum with the thalamus, a central relay station located in the midbrain.

This was an extremely tricky operation, however. The cut had to be made in exactly the right place to bring relief of the symptoms without seriously damaging other important brain structures. Among one hundred patients, thirty-nine obtained relief without any side effects; but some of the others were paralyzed, and seventeen died. Other surgeons also tried similar operations around the same time, but many of their patients suffered seizures or paralysis. Therefore, the treatment did not seem very promising.

The development of a technique called stereotactic surgery made the operation practical. X-ray films made it possible to locate the nerve cell

Dr. Russell Meyers made an interesting discovery in 1939. He found that he could relieve his patient's tremor and rigidity by making a cut in the corpus stratum.

bundle precisely. Then, a needle was inserted and an electric current was sent through it right to the bundle, cutting the nerve cells. Henry Wycis and Ernst Spiegel built a stereotactic setup in 1947 for this delicate brain surgery. During the 1950s, they treated seventy Parkinson's patients and reported successful relief of symptoms in 70 percent.

These surgeons also developed a way of making sure they were cutting the right cells before any permanent damage was done. They injected procaine, an anesthetic, into the suspected bundle of nerve cells. The patient, who was awake during the brain surgery, could tell them immediately when the symptoms were relieved. Other surgeons introduced further refinements, and thousands of operations were performed. New York surgeon Irving S. Cooper, for example, used cryosurgery, with a probe cooled by liquid nitrogen, to kill the nerve cells by freezing them. In some cases, however, the surgery resulted in a paralyzing stroke or left the patient with speech or movement problems. Moreover, surgery helped only tremor and stiffness, but not accompanying symptoms.[17]

Medical experts are still looking for better ways to treat Parkinson's disease. They hope that future treatments may even permanently repair the damage and bring patients back to normal.

3

What is Parkinson's Disease?

J anet Reno has always been a fighter—someone who does not give up when faced with difficulties. When she entered law school in 1960, she was one of just sixteen women in a class of five hundred. After she received her degree, one of the biggest law firms in Miami refused to hire her because she was a woman. But she persevered, building a successful career in a field that was dominated by men. Fourteen years later, she became a partner in the same law firm that had originally turned her down. Meanwhile, she had served in 1971 as director of the judiciary committee of the Florida House of Representatives and helped to revise the court system in Florida.

In 1973, while working in the Dade County State Attorney's Office, Reno pioneered in organizing a juvenile division for the Miami area. In 1978, she became State Attorney for Dade County. There, she set up a special unit to help police arrest and convict repeat offenders. This unit also focused on prevention programs to help keep children from getting involved in gangs, drugs, and violence. Dade County voters, who reelected her four successive times, were not surprised when President Clinton nominated her as Attorney General of the United States in 1993.[1] She was the first woman ever appointed to that position.

As Attorney General, Reno impressed Americans with her blunt, no-nonsense approach. She has dealt with her personal life in the same way, especially when she found out that she had a serious medical condition.

In the summer of 1995, Janet Reno noticed that her left hand was shaking. She didn't think much about it, figuring it would go away. When the shaking continued, she saw a doctor. The

Attorney General Janet Reno was diagnosed with Parkinson's disease in the summer of 1995.

diagnosis was Parkinson's disease. The doctor felt that she was in a mild, early stage of the disease and promptly began treatment with medications. A combination of two drugs brought the tremors under control.

In her typically straightforward manner, Reno announced her condition to the public in a news conference in November, 1995. Some of the reporters were not completely surprised; they had noticed the trembling even before Reno did and had asked earlier in the year whether she had a health problem. Reno's colleagues in the Justice Department had also noticed the trembling. Some people were concerned about her ability to continue doing her job. Reno had no doubts. "I feel fine now," she said firmly. "I don't feel I have any impairment."[2]

Three years after her diagnosis, Janet Reno's condition worsened. She was classified as stage 2 on a scale of 1 to 5 (5 being most severe). The shaking had progressed to both sides of her body, and the tremors were very noticeable. On May 7, 1999, Reno joined rock performers at an MTV event to promote a CD-ROM against youth violence. At one point, the tremors that affected both her arms were so severe that both the podium and microphone shook. She even shook in her seat, but unlike most Parkinson's patients, Reno didn't employ any tricks to hide her symptoms—she just folded her hands in her lap in plain sight.[3] The same thing happened in August, 1999 at the annual convention for the American Bar Association's House of Delegates. As Reno spoke to the Bar Association's group, she could not control her hands. Her left arm bobbed up and down, while the fingers on her right hand moved aimlessly in the air.[4] But Reno's appearance has not changed her image for those who admire her. MTV president Judy McGrath commented on what she saw during

Reno's appearance, "I see it. I feel bad for a minute and I completely forget about it. When Reno works a crowd, people look her in the eye, not at her hands. If anything, you respect her even more."[5]

G. Robert Witmer, Jr., a lawyer who attended the convention for the Bar Association, had great admiration for Reno. "I think she is very brave," he said. "I think it actually enhances the delivery of her message to see someone who is coping with a physical disability and not letting it deter her from her job."[6] Although dealing with such a debilitating disease can be very difficult, especially because she was constantly in the public eye while she was Attorney General, Janet Reno has refused to let the disease keep her from doing her job and living her life.

Who Gets Parkinson's?

Janet Reno unwittingly became a role model for people with Parkinson's. The disease generally affects people over the age of fifty. Reno's case is typical. She was fifty-seven years old at the time of diagnosis—the average age of onset of PD.[7] An estimated 1.5 million people in the United States are affected by Parkinson's disease. And roughly 50,000 new cases are reported each year.[8] More people suffer from Parkinson's disease than from multiple sclerosis and muscular dystrophy combined.[9]

But Parkinson's is not strictly a disease of the middle-aged and elderly, as many people think. About 10 percent of people with Parkinson's develop symptoms before the age of fifty. Michael J. Fox is a perfect example of this young-onset Parkinson's, as it is called. Fox has helped increase public

A Very Young Parkinson's Patient

When Michael J. Fox went public about his Parkinson's condition, people were shocked that such a young person could develop this "aging disease." But he is far from the youngest case ever observed.

Emily Hamilton's parents didn't think it was a major problem when they noticed that Emily's feet turned inward, which is common among three-and-a-half-year-olds. But her toes curled under when she walked. When she was five, her handwriting, which had been good, deteriorated greatly. Her printing went from smooth lines and curves to a scrawl. She also started to have trouble walking.

Emily's symptoms would fluctuate. When she first woke up each day, she could walk and write normally. But by late morning, her symptoms would worsen and she would have trouble doing these simple activities. By nighttime, Emily would not be able to walk at all. She could only crawl. She developed other symptoms, as well. Both of her hands would shake, and her left arm stayed bent at the elbow, while her left leg was rigidly bent at the knee.

Doctors could not explain Emily's condition. No childhood disorders seemed to fit her symptoms. She went through a variety of tests until doctors finally diagnosed Parkinson's disease, a disease that normally affects adults.

Once Emily was treated with medication, most of her symptoms disappeared, but her health will be in question as she grows up.[10]

awareness about PD, showing that this is a serious disease that can affect the young as well as the old.[11]

Parkinson's disease can occur anywhere in the world, although its prevalence can vary greatly. It can occur in both men and women, but men tend to have a slightly higher incidence.

How the Brain Works

Parkinson's disease is a disease of the central nervous system (CNS), which includes the brain and the spinal cord (the control and coordination centers of the body). The spinal cord carries messages to and from the brain. But if certain parts of the brain are damaged, messages cannot be sent effectively, and serious problems can develop. Therefore, in order to understand what goes wrong in Parkinson's, we need to learn a little about the brain and how it works.

Everything about us—our memories, thoughts, plans, attitudes, and personality—is stored in the brain. The largest part of the brain, with which we think, remember, make decisions, and control the movements of the body, is called the cerebrum. Actually, most of this activity takes place in the cerebral cortex, the outermost layer of the brain. This layer, less than 3/4 inch (6 millimeters) thick, contains billions of neurons, which receive messages from different parts of the body or from other areas of the brain and send out messages to control the activities of the body. Different groups of neurons have different jobs. Sensory neurons carry messages to the brain from the eyes, ears, nose, tongue, and other sense receptors to the CNS. Without them, we could not see a bird flying, hear a train whistle, smell or taste a sizzling steak, or feel the roundness of an apple with our fingers.

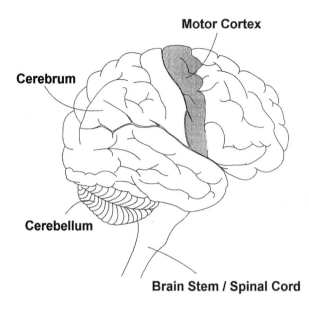

Motor Cortex

Cerebrum

Cerebellum

Brain Stem / Spinal Cord

Messages that move muscles begin in the motor cortex of the cerebrum.

Motor neurons carry messages from the brain and spinal cord to the muscles of the body, the glands, and various other structures. These neurons help people to walk and run, throw a ball, write a letter, and even chew their food. Each neuron carries messages to or from the brain—never both ways.

Neurons transmit messages in the body through electrical signals. Each neuron is specially made for receiving and sending these signals. A single neuron consists of a cell body with many threadlike fibers extending from it. The neuron sends information to other nerve cells through a single, long, hair-like fiber called an axon that extends from the cell body. The other threadlike fibers extending from the cell body are called dendrites. They look like the branches of a tree. Dendrites receive information

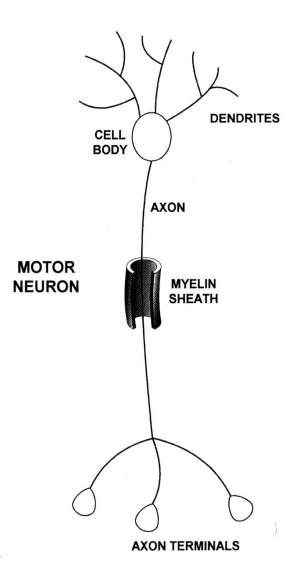

Neurons transmit messages in the body through electrical signals. The neuron sends information to other nerve cells through the axon and to the dendrites, where the message is relayed to the next motor neuron.

from other nerve cells. Each axon ends in a cluster of tiny branches called terminals. Each axon terminal can relay messages to another nerve cell, although the two cells are not directly in contact. (A tiny, fluid-filled gap called a synapse separates the axon terminal from the dendrite of the neighboring neuron.)

How does a nerve message get across the synapse between the axon of one neuron and the dendrite of another? When a neuron is stimulated, an electrical charge travels along it to the axon terminals. These terminals release special chemicals (neurotransmitters), which float through the fluid in the synapses to the dendrites of the next neurons in the chain. Each of these neurons picks up the neurotransmitter on a special structure called a receptor, suitable to react chemically with just that neurotransmitter. When dendrite receptors pick up neurotransmitters, the neuron is stimulated in turn. Then an electrical charge travels along it to its axon terminals, where more neurotransmitters can be released to pass the message on to other nerve cells or to stimulate muscle cells to contract. Within the brain, various control and coordination centers continually exchange information by nerve messages relayed in this way along interlocking chains of neurons.

Two of the main neurotransmitters in the brain are acetylcholine and dopamine. Messages carried along nerve-cell pathways that use acetylcholine stimulate nerve and muscle-cell activity. Dopamine, on the other hand, inhibits, or turns off, nerve cell activity in most parts of the brain. Normally, there is a constant interaction between the acetylcholine- and dopamine-carried messages, so that they remain in a fine-tuned balance. This kind of interaction among the nerve centers in the brain that control muscle activity is what makes smooth, controlled movements possible.

Many parts of the brain are involved in controlling and coordinating muscle movements. Two narrow strips running down the sides of the cerebral cortex are called the motor strips. These are the neurons whose messages start off and help to control intentional, voluntary movements. A specific portion of each motor strip corresponds to each part of the body—the hand, the foot, or the tongue, for example. Curiously enough, the brain is "wired" in a crisscross fashion, so that the motor cortex in the left side of the brain controls movements in the right side of the body, and vice versa.

The motor cortex is linked by networks of neurons to some other important motor control centers, located deep within the brain in the basal ganglia. One of the most important parts of the basal ganglia is the corpus striatum, or striatum. The striatum continually receives information about body position and movement from the parts of the brain where messages from the sense organs are received and analyzed. A simple walk across the room is actually a very complicated process. The brain has to figure out where the feet are, and how big the steps should be to keep the body from toppling over. All these computations are done very quickly in the striatum. The striatum also helps to maintain good muscle tone, and it remembers the instructions for performing learned muscle activities (like riding a bike or tying a shoe) and carries them out automatically. During all these complex tasks, the parts of the corpus striatum "talk to each other" by way of acetylcholine-carried messages. Links with the substantia nigra, another part of the basal ganglia that sends inhibitory dopamine messages to the corpus striatum, help to control and coordinate the motor activity.[12]

The motor centers in the basal ganglia are also linked with various structures of the limbic system, parts of the brain involved in emotions and reactions. Messages from the limbic system can make a person want to perform a particular action. Another key part of the motor control system is the cerebellum, located at the lower back of the brain. In the cerebellum, movements and positions of body parts are continuously monitored, and adjustments are made. The action of the cerebellum, for example, keeps you from "overshooting" and knocking over your glass of milk when you are reaching out to pick up your spoon.[13]

What Happens in Parkinson's?

Normally, the substantial nigra produces large amounts of dopamine. But in Parkinson's, the dopamine-producing cells are damaged and die, reducing the production of dopamine. Without enough dopamine, there cannot be a flow of inhibitory messages to control the activity of the brain centers that stimulate muscle movements. The flow of acetylcholine-carried messages continues, however, and the result may be tremors or a continuous contraction of muscles, producing rigidity. The disruption of the coordinated interplay of inhibition and stimulation can also result in "freezing," so that the person finds it very difficult to move at all.

The loss of dopamine-producing cells is a gradual process. During the early stages of the disease, a large percentage of cells die, but the damage is not severe enough to cause trouble. That is because the remaining neurons take over the work of the

Telltale Signs

What is the difference between Parkinson's disease and other types of parkinsonism? Many scientists would answer: Lewy bodies. Lewy bodies are abnormal microscopic structures found within damaged nerve cells in the substantial nigra and other areas of the brain. They can be seen only in an autopsy.

Although Lewy bodies can be found in other diseases, they are considered to be the hallmark of Parkinson's disease. In fact, many neurologists tend to follow the rule: "If there are no Lewy bodies, it is not Parkinson's disease." Lewy bodies are not present in other types of parkinsonism.

Sometimes, however, Lewy bodies can be found in elderly people who did not show any signs of Parkinson's disease before they died. That means that these people probably had Parkinson's disease, and would have eventually developed symptoms if they had lived longer. Thus, a number of people may have the disease and not even know it.[15] Interestingly, however, doctors have found that about 25 percent of PD patients did not have any Lewy bodies after they died even though they had been diagnosed with Parkinson's disease.[16]

damaged ones. As more and more neurons die, however, the need for dopamine becomes more than the remaining neurons can handle. When the dopamine level is decreased by 60 to 80 percent, the first symptoms start to develop.[14]

What Are the Symptoms?

When James Parkinson first described Parkinson's disease, he listed a group of symptoms that doctors still use today (with the addition of rigidity). A group of symptoms that generally occur together in a particular disease is often referred to as a syndrome. So the typical collection of symptoms of Parkinson's disease is also called Parkinson's syndrome, or simply parkinsonism.

Parkinson's disease is a progressive disease—the symptoms worsen gradually over time. A person with Parkinson's may experience mild symptoms for five to ten years before it gets worse. Symptoms can vary greatly among PD patients. Although there are some common symptoms, some people may have certain symptoms and not others. Some PD patients even have symptoms that most patients do not have. In addition, various factors may influence the severity of the symptoms. Stress, for instance, can worsen Parkinsonian symptoms.

Symptoms may also be unpredictable. The patient's symptoms may develop during breakfast, for instance, then suddenly disappear later on in the day.

Signs that are characteristic of Parkinson's disease are known as primary symptoms. They include the following:

- *Tremors at rest*—Tremors, or shaking back and forth, occur when the limbs are relaxed. Resting tremors develop in about 75 percent of PD patients. Tremors start out on one side of the body,

Characteristic symptoms of Parkinson's are a stooped-over posture, a slow-moving gait, and hand tremors that are known as pill-rolling.

usually in one hand, and later spread to the other side. Tremors may also occur in the feet or legs, as well as the lips and jaw. Shaking in the head and neck, however, are not typical. Resting tremors usually disappear during sleep or improve with voluntary movement. Hand tremors may appear as "pill-rolling," in which the person rubs the forefinger against the thumb.

- *Rigidity*—Parkinson's patients may experience stiffness in their limbs. Normally, muscles need to relax and contract for a person's arms and legs to move smoothly. But in PD, the muscles tighten up and stay contracted and the limbs are unable to move. This state of persistent muscle contraction may cause aching, stiffness, weakness, and jerky movements.

- *Slowness of movement*—Also known as bradykinesia, this is a slowing or loss of automatic movement. It is particularly frustrating because it can happen unpredictably. At any given time, the patient can suddenly lose the ability to move around and may need help walking or getting out of a chair. The patient can take hours to perform simple tasks, such as taking a shower or getting dressed.

- *Impaired balance and coordination*—PD patients may have trouble keeping their balance, and may fall easily. The condition may also result in a stooped-over posture. As the disease progresses, walking may be affected. Patients may try to walk really fast, taking several tiny steps, in order to keep their balance. This is called festination.

41

- *Freezing*—Patients may stop suddenly and "freeze," unable to move at all, and may fall over. Freezing can affect any movements, such as finger tapping or the muscle movements involved in speech. It can be especially upsetting when it affects walking. Patients say it feels as though their feet were stuck to the floor.

Symptoms that occur in less than 50 percent of PD patients are known as secondary symptoms. They include:

- *Dementia*—Disorientation, confusion and memory loss; it occurs in 30 percent of patients.

- *Depression*—Often occurs in PD patients; as many as 50 percent of patients need to be treated with antidepressant medication.

- *Facial masking*—Occurs when facial muscles experience both rigidity and bradykinesia. The patient's face appears blank, without any expression.

- *Difficulty in swallowing and chewing*—Food and saliva may collect at the back of the mouth because swallowing muscles do not work. This may cause choking or drooling.

- *Speech problems*—PD patients may speak very softly or in a monotone voice. Or they may speak too quickly, hesitate before speaking, or repeat or slur their words.

- *Urinary problems or constipation*—PD patients may lose bladder control or may be unable to urinate. Bowel muscles also may have trouble functioning normally, resulting in constipation.

Following the Progress of Parkinson's Disease

Parkinson's symptoms are classified into five stages. As the symptoms worsen, the patient's condition starts with a mild stage 1 and gradually progresses through the stages. The most severe condition is classified as stage 5, but many patients may delay this stage, thanks to modern treatments.

Stage 1:
- Symptoms are mild.
- Signs and symptoms appear on only one side of the body.
- Symptoms are annoying, but not disabling.
- Tremors usually develop in only one limb.

Stage 2:
- Symptoms develop on both sides of the body.
- Symptoms cause slight disability.
- Problems in posture and walking.

Stage 3:
- Body movements are greatly slowed.
- Symptoms cause major problems with functioning normally.
- Balance is impaired.

Stage 4:
- Symptoms are severe.
- The patient can still walk, but with great difficulty.
- Symptoms of rigidity and slowness of movement worsen.
- Patient needs help to do everyday activities.

Stage 5:
- Patient becomes bedridden or confined to a wheelchair, and needs constant care.[18]

- *Skin problems*—PD patients may develop very oily or dry skin on the face.

- *Sleep problems*—PD patients may experience problems sleeping.

- *Handwriting problems*—Handwriting may appear small and crowded.[17]

Scientists know that the symptoms of Parkinson's disease are due to a drop in the dopamine production in certain areas of the brain. But what causes these cells to stop producing enough dopamine? In most cases, this is not yet known. Doctors call these cases idiopathic Parkinson's disease. The term *idiopathic* means "of unknown cause." This condition is also sometimes called primary parkinsonism. Some forms of parkinsonism do have a variety of known causes. These conditions are classified as secondary parkinsonism.

4

What Causes Parkinson's Disease?

Constantin von Economo, an Austrian neurologist, was puzzled about a viral epidemic he was studying. It had affected roughly five million people throughout the world since it first appeared around 1918 and mysteriously disappeared in the 1920s. The virus caused a disease known as encephalitis, or inflammation of the brain. Because one of its main symptoms was a coma-like state of sleepiness, the encephalitis epidemic was known as *encephalitis lethargica*. In the United States, where it claimed the lives of one-third of its victims, it was commonly called "sleeping sickness."

Patients who survived suffered devastating effects from the disease. Many went into a deep sleep, unable to be awakened. Other symptoms and signs included a fever, headache, difficulty swallowing, tremors, a stiffness in the neck and back, and other problems. Many people—but not all—who had recovered successfully developed a strange new condition weeks, months,

Australian neurologist Constantin von Economo studied a viral epidemic known as encephalitis.

or even years later. Scientists called this new syndrome postencephalitic parkinsonism because its symptoms were remarkably similar to those of idiopathic Parkinson's disease. Tremors, for instance, were a major feature in both conditions. In addition, some patients with postencephalitic parkinsonism became catatonic; they stayed in a frozen-like state, unable to move or talk. But there were also some major differences between these two conditions. Cases of postencephalitic parkinsonism usually involved young victims, between the ages of fifteen and thirty, whereas PD patients were rarely under forty years old. Postencephalitic parkinsonism also progressed at a much slower rate than Parkinson's disease. Patients showed some symptoms that were not seen in Parkinson's patients, such as obsessive-compulsiveness, and their eyes turned up as though they were looking toward the ceiling.[1]

During the mid-1960s, Dr. Oliver Sacks studied a group of patients with sleeping sickness at the Beth Abraham Hospital in New York. These patients had spent decades in catatonic, frozen states, unable to make voluntary movements. They looked like statues. In 1969, Dr. Sacks treated these patients with the then-experimental drug L-dopa. The results were extraordinary. The patients went through a kind of "awakening." Suddenly, they could move, they could talk, and they could eat. They were able to leave the hospital and take field trips into New York City for the first time in years. Unfortunately, the effects of L-dopa on these patients did not last long, and they eventually returned to their original condition.

Dr. Sacks wrote about his work with these patients in his book, *Awakenings*, published in 1973. In 1990, this book was made into a critically acclaimed movie starring Robert DeNiro and Robin Williams.[2]

Scientists still do not know what virus caused the development of postencephalitic parkinsonism. Because it is no longer infecting anyone, it is highly unlikely that they will ever find out.

This historical account has suggested that idiopathic Parkinson's disease may be caused by a virus, as well. There is no evidence,

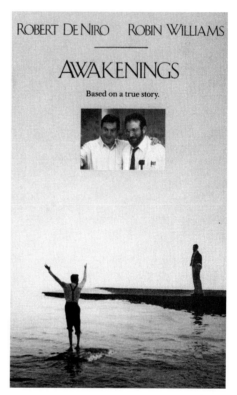

The movie *Awakenings,* starring Robin Williams and Robert DeNiro, is based on the book Dr. Oliver Sacks wrote about his experiences treating patients with L-dopa.

however, to confirm this belief. Scientists have come up with a number of other possible theories on the causes of Parkinson's disease.

Drug-Induced Parkinsonism

Certain drugs may produce symptoms of parkinsonism, especially among the elderly. Such drugs include chlorpromazine and haloperidol, which are used to treat psychiatric disorders; metoclopramide, prescribed for stomach disorders; and reserpine, used to treat high blood pressure. These kinds of drugs apparently reduce the production of neurotransmitters, including dopamine, in the brain and therefore produce Parkinson's-like symptoms. Fortunately, drug-induced parkinsonism is reversible. The symptoms will disappear a few weeks or months after the patient stops taking the medication. The symptoms could also disappear if the dosage is reduced.[3]

Head Trauma

At the start of the 1996 summer Olympics in Atlanta, millions of people were moved as they watched Muhammad Ali, the former world heavyweight boxing champion and a 1960 Olympic gold medal winner, take the torch. Holding it carefully in his trembling hands, he reached out to light the Olympic flame. It was heartbreaking to see how parkinsonism had taken its toll on this tremendous icon since he was first diagnosed with this condition in the mid-1980s. During his boxing days, Ali boasted proudly that he could "float like a butterfly, sting like a bee," but now it was a struggle just to stand without stumbling and hold the torch out to the flame.[4]

During his boxing days, Muhammad Ali boasted that he could "float like a butterfly, sting like a bee," but by the mid-1980s, it became a struggle for him to even stand.

Some scientists believe that Muhammad Ali does not actually have true Parkinson's disease. They say that he has a type of Parkinson's syndrome called pugilistic parkinsonism. This is a condition that can affect boxers who receive a number of blows to the head that cause damage to the brain. Parkinsonian symptoms, such as tremors, muscle stiffness, and loss of muscle control, tend to worsen even after the boxer stops fighting. Some medical experts believe that a boxer who gets knocked out a significant number of times may have an increased risk of developing parkinsonism.

Imagine what happens to a boxer's brain during a fight. Normally, the brain floats inside the skull. When a boxer gets hit in the head, the brain crashes against the skull, which may cause some amount of nerve cell damage. If the blows to the head occur repeatedly, the damage could add up to significant brain damage. Eventually, the brain starts to break down, and the boxer loses the ability to function normally. This brain damage could lead to parkinsonism. Some medical experts believe that pugilistic parkinsonism also affected other world-famous boxers, like Jack Dempsey and Joe Louis.[5]

Other medical experts, however, do not believe that Ali's condition was caused by head trauma that resulted from boxing. In 1997, Ali's physician, Dr. Mahlon De Long, chair of neurology at Emery University in Atlanta, said that he felt that Ali does have true Parkinson's disease because his symptoms respond very well to levodopa, the medication used to treat PD.[6]

Genetic Factors

Some scientists believe that genes may somehow be involved in the development of Parkinson's disease. It is possible, they say, that a defective gene may make certain people more sensitive to toxins in the environment, such as metals or pesticides. Their body responds by speeding up the destruction of nerve cells in the substantial nigra.

In an effort to prove this theory, early studies were conducted using twins, who share a genetic makeup. One study involved forty-three pairs of identical twins and nineteen pairs of fraternal (not genetically identical) twins, in which one of the twins had PD. It was found that in only one case of identical twins did both twins develop PD. These original twin studies thus did not provide confirming evidence of genetic involvement.[7] It is not easy trying to demonstrate a genetic link in a disease that develops late in life, however. Adults, even identical twins, are exposed to different experiences throughout their lives. Other factors may be involved.

Nonetheless, scientists continued their search for a genetic link in Parkinson's. Recently, a major breakthrough occurred when scientists studied the occurrence of PD in a very large family, who originated from the village of Contursi in southern Italy. Records showed that 592 members of this family were all descended from a common ancestor who lived eleven generations before. Researchers found out that over the past four generations,

A breakthrough recently occurred when scientists studied the occurrence of Parkinson's disease in a very large family.

sixty-one members of this family have shown symptoms of Parkinson's disease. Half of these people lived in Italy all their lives; the other half lived in the United States, mainly around New York City. In two of the cases, a confirmation of Parkinson's disease was made after autopsies revealed the presence of Lewy bodies in the substantial nigra.[8]

The study of this Italian family led to a landmark discovery. In June 1997, researchers at the National Human Genome Research Institute (NEGRI) announced that they had evidence identifying a defective gene on chromosome 4q that could lead to Parkinson's disease in some families. They also found the same genetic defect in five smaller Greek families. The gene to blame directs the production of alpha-synuclein, a protein found in nerve cells in the brain. It is not known why this defective protein causes Parkinson's disease, but it apparently plays an important part in the development or behavior of Lewy bodies.[9]

In studies of other families, scientists have identified other defective gene locations that can also cause Parkinson's. For instance, in 1993, it was reported that a family from Sioux City, Iowa, had twenty-two members with Parkinson's disease over five generations. Autopsies of several family members found Lewy bodies, confirming that it was true Parkinson's disease.[10] Recently, it was discovered that this family had a defective gene located on chromosome 4p.[11]

Presently, genetic mutations account for only a small number of PD cases worldwide. Still, scientists believe that this finding is a huge step in Parkinson's research. They now have a genetic model for Parkinson's and they hope to use this knowledge for further research.[12]

Environmental Toxins

Some medical historians believe that because James Parkinson first described Parkinson's disease around the start of the Industrial Revolution, it seems reasonable to believe that environmental toxins may be to blame for the development of the disease. It is possible that the "overdose" or buildup of chemicals may cause an eventual breakdown in the functioning of the brain's nerve cells, thus causing PD.

The belief that environmental toxins may cause PD was strengthened by some strange events during the late 1970s and early 1980s.

A young man who was addicted to drugs set up his own laboratory in his home in Arlington, Virginia. In 1977, the man tried following a chemical recipe from a medical journal in hopes of creating a synthetic form of Demerol (a painkiller). The man rushed through the experiment, anxious to try out his creation. But the results were disastrous. He soon became severely ill, rigid, and unable to move. He was in a frozen-like state and had to be taken to the hospital. A doctor there thought that the man's symptoms sounded a lot like Parkinson's. The man was treated with an antiparkinson drug, and his severe symptoms improved. But a short time later, his symptoms returned.

The young man was then referred to the National Institutes of Health (NIH) at Bethesda, Maryland. Doctors at the NIH tried to follow the man's recipe, and soon discovered that the man had unintentionally produced a byproduct because the chemical reaction had been heated too much. The doctors found out that the chemical makeup of the byproduct was called 1-methyl-4-phenyl-1,2,3,6-tetrahydropyridine, or MPTP.

53

A group of scientists at the NIH, headed by Dr. Irving Kopin, tested the effects of MPTP on monkeys in the laboratory. They discovered that the monkeys developed Parkinson's-like symptoms after they were injected with tiny amounts of MPTP. Even with such small amounts, the monkeys became rigid and unable to move. A dose of levodopa helped relieve the symptoms. An hour later, however, their symptoms returned, just like what had happened to the young man. The researchers also found an accumulation of a byproduct of MPTP, known as 1-methyl-4-phenyl-4-hydroxypiperidine (or MPP+), in the brains of these monkeys. It was not yet clear what effect MPP+ had on the brain.

The young man continued to be treated for his severe Parkinsonian symptoms, but within a year he died of a drug overdose. Doctors performed an autopsy and found that the nerve cells of the substantial nigra were completely destroyed. Researchers found that the same thing occurred in the experimental animals, as well.

In 1979, a group of doctors published a detailed description of the young man's tragic experience. Unfortunately, this report went unnoticed until 1982, when several heroin addicts ended up in a California emergency room after injecting themselves with an illegal drug they had bought off the streets. These drug addicts exhibited severe Parkinson's-like symptoms: rigidity, shakiness, slow movements, and stooped-over postures. Some were in a frozen-like state, unable to move. Luckily, a technician from the poison control center realized that these patients seemed remarkably similar to the young man from Virginia. Neurologist Dr. J. William Langston was then brought in to run tests on a sample of the drug that the addicts had taken. The tests showed that the drug contained MPTP.[13]

Experiments were conducted on monkeys to study the effects of MPTP on the brain. The monkeys did indeed develop parkinsonism after being injected with MPTP, and the nerve cells in the substantial nigra were destroyed. Soon, researchers all over the world were studying MPTP, hoping that it might hold the key to the cause of Parkinson's disease and could lead to better treatments.

Within a few years, scientists found out why MPTP produces a Parkinson's-like condition in its victims. Apparently, MPTP by itself is not dangerous. But when this chemical enters the body, it goes through some changes when it comes into contact with an enzyme known as monoamine oxidase B, or MAO B. (An enzyme is a protein that helps chemical reactions to proceed, without being changed itself in the process.) Interestingly, this enzyme breaks down dopamine after it is released in the brain. MAO B reacts with MPTP and changes it into a toxic substance, MPP+, which destroys nerve cells in the substantial nigra.[14]

Scientists also discovered that a drug called deprenyl (or selegiline) can inhibit or block MAO B and keep it from producing MPP+. Dr. Richard Heikkila from the Robert Wood Johnson Medical School in New Brunswick, New Jersey, found that when mice were given an MAO B inhibitor before they received a dose of MPTP, they did not develop parkinsonism. In mice that received MPTP without the MAO inhibitor, however, the nerve cells of the substantial nigra were destroyed. Dr. Langston and his colleagues conducted similar experiments with monkeys and observed the same results. Some medical experts believe that deprenyl may slow the progression of Parkinsonian symptoms if it is taken soon after the diagnosis—the earlier the better. MPTP has proven to be an important model for Parkinson's disease. Unfortunately, unlike drug-induced parkinsonism, which is a temporary condition, the damage caused by MPTP is permanent.

The similarities between true Parkinson's and MPTP-induced parkinsonism are so remarkable that some scientists believe that a similar kind of substance occurring in nature or even man-made chemicals, such as pesticides, that pollute the environment, might be a cause of Parkinson's disease. In fact, many pesticides and herbicides contain chemicals that are related to MPP+,[15] and people who live or work on farms have up to seven times the average risk of developing PD. In 2000, researchers at Emory University in Atlanta reported that the

Many pesticides and herbicides contain chemicals that are related to MPP+. People who live or work on farms have up to seven times the average risk of developing Parkinson's disease.

widely used pesticide rotenone produced classic Parkinson's symptoms in experimental rats, including tremors and stiffness. Their brains showed a progressive destruction of dopamine-producing neurons, and Lewy bodies were observed.[16] Some scientists also believe that another environmental toxin, aluminum, may increase the risk of developing Parkinson's. The metal has been found in abnormally high concentration in the substantial nigra of PD patients.[17]

There are some problems with the environmental-link theory, however. For instance, why is it that only one person in a family may develop PD when all the family members live in the same environment and are exposed to the same toxins? Many scientists now believe that it is likely that most cases of Parkinson's disease are caused by a combined genetic tendency and exposure to an environmental toxin.

Oxidative Damage

Chemical reactions are going on in our bodies all the time. Nutrients from foods are processed in various ways, using them as building blocks for constructing complex body chemicals or "burning" them to release energy to fuel the body's activities. In other reactions, various body chemicals are taken apart, or added to, or react with one another. All these reactions are aided by enzymes. Oxygen from the air we breathe is necessary for the energy-releasing reactions, which take place in the mitochondria (specialized structures inside the body cells). Chemists refer to the energy-releasing reactions as oxidative reactions. (The enzymes that help them to go—like MAO—are called oxidases.)

One of the key findings in the study of MPTP was that MPP+ kills nerve cells by poisoning the mitochondria. Inside these structures, MPP+ interferes with an enzyme system called "complex 1," which helps run the energy-releasing oxidation reactions. The mitochondria then cannot supply energy, and the nerve cells die. Evidence such as this has prompted some scientists to suggest that the key to Parkinson's disease lies in the oxidative reactions that dopamine undergoes in the brain. Hydrogen peroxide is one of the products of these reactions. It is a rather unstable chemical that can break down into very reactive free radicals. Free radicals can also be produced in biological substances by other influences, such as radiation. They can do a lot of damage as they bounce into various complex body chemicals, breaking them apart or linking them together into sludgy masses. Normally, the body's protective mechanisms can prevent the formation of free radicals. But if too much hydrogen peroxide is formed for the body's defenses to handle, free radicals are produced.

There is a lot of evidence to support the idea that oxidative reactions and free radicals play an important role in Parkinson's. Patients have been found to have much less than normal amounts of several protective chemicals, and higher amounts of oxidation-promoting substances in the substantial nigra—a situation that does not exist in patients with other disorders. Researchers have also found higher-than-normal levels of oxidized forms of brain chemicals in the substantial nigra of Parkinson's patients.[18] And when Parkinson's disease was produced in monkeys, it was found that another protective substance decreased rapidly in their brains.[19]

The idea that "oxidative stress"—an excess of oxidative reactions in the brain, leading to the formation of free radicals—may be a cause of Parkinson's suggests a possible approach to preventing the disease or slowing its progression. Vitamin C, vitamin E, and various other chemicals that are found in foods are natural antioxidants (substances that protect body chemicals from oxidative reactions and the potentially harmful free radicals they generate). There is some preliminary evidence that taking supplements of antioxidants, particularly vitamin C, can slow the progression of Parkinson's disease.[20] Limiting the intake of metals such as iron and aluminum might also have a protective effect. Advice on measures to take to prevent the disease, however, are still very tentative and will remain so until more definite evidence of its causes is available. Meanwhile, medical efforts are focused mainly on the treatment of its symptoms and helping patients to live a more normal life.

5

Diagnosing Parkinson's Disease

Alan, a fifty-four-year-old executive, was not feeling quite himself as he was getting ready for a big sales presentation. His hands were trembling as he sat quietly at his desk. Alan figured it was just nerves or fatigue. He had been feeling overly tired lately and rather depressed. He did not pay too much attention to it, assuming it was due to the pressure at work. But when the shaking, depression, and fatigue continued, Alan decided to see a doctor.

Alan's doctor ran a variety of tests, including blood work, chest X-rays, and urinalysis. The doctor also asked Alan all sorts of questions concerning his daily routine, work conditions, stress, and even his diet. Because Alan was depressed, his doctor referred him to a psychiatrist. Over the next six or seven months, the psychiatrist prescribed antidepressants, which only made Alan feel worse. Alan then went to a neurologist, who after examining him, remarked, "Well, it doesn't look like Parkinson's disease anyway." This could have been because Alan's symptoms were not as noticeable as those of other Parkinson's patients, and the tremors were never obvious when he went to the doctor. Alan eventually saw two other neurologists within the next year, until Parkinson's disease was finally diagnosed.[1]

Beth, a sixty-eight-year-old retired schoolteacher, noticed that she was getting tired more easily than she used to. She moved around a lot more slowly, and it took her a while to get simple things done. She could not even enjoy doing gardening work. It had now become painful to do such tasks. "I thought it was just the price I had to pay for getting on in years," Beth said. But when her husband noticed that Beth was dragging her right leg, he became worried. He told her that she also seemed to stare out into space a lot, and hardly ever smiled anymore. When Beth herself started to notice that she was having problems walking, she knew something was wrong. So she went to see a doctor.

The doctor believed almost from the start that Beth's symptoms suggested Parkinson's disease. But just to be sure, she had to go through a variety of tests to rule out other conditions whose symptoms may resemble those of PD. After examining the patient, studying the tests, and collecting information from Beth, the doctor confirmed a diagnosis of Parkinson's disease.[2]

Confusing the Signs

Parkinson's disease is a disease of aging—a condition that typically affects older people. The problem is that people tend to expect their bodies to slow down as they age. They may consider

Parkinson's or Essential Tremor?

Parkinson's disease is often linked with images of a person who shakes a lot. But there are actually a number of other illnesses that involve tremors. For instance, a condition called essential tremor is often confused with the more serious illness, Parkinson's disease. Essential tremor is a progressive neurological disorder, which may occur in the elderly or the young and gradually worsens over time. This condition often runs in families. It is more common than Parkinson's, affecting four to six million people in the United States.

Like Parkinson's, tremors are a hallmark of essential tremor (hence its name). But these two conditions have some very important differences. For instance, essential tremor usually occurs during activity. The tremors of Parkinson's, however, often occur while the body is at rest (although they can occur at any time). In addition, shaking hands may occur in both diseases, but essential tremor may develop in the head and voice, which is rare in Parkinson's.

Essential tremor does not have any real link to Parkinson's disease. Both diseases usually respond differently to drugs. But it is estimated that 5 to 10 percent of people with essential tremor eventually develop Parkinson's disease.[3]

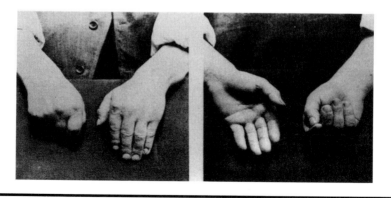

signs of shakiness or feeling unsteady as part of the normal aging process. That is why many people may confuse signs of Parkinson's disease with simply "getting older." Since parkinsonian symptoms tend to develop gradually, it is not easy to notice that something is wrong.

In addition, many older people take medications to treat conditions such as high blood pressure. And certain medications may cause Parkinson's-like symptoms. This could lead to a misdiagnosis.

Doctors may also have problems diagnosing PD because the symptoms may be not be obvious or can be vague, such as in Alan's case. For instance, depression often occurs in Parkinson's patients, so doctors may confuse that sign with clinical depression. Signs of fatigue and shakiness could also be caused by a number of other conditions.

There is no blood test or X-ray that can confirm a diagnosis of Parkinson's disease. A neurologist has to base the patient's diagnosis on a physical exam, background information, and laboratory tests that can rule out other conditions. Sometimes, doctors may diagnose a patient with Parkinson's by the way he or she responds to antiparkinson medication.

Collect Information

There are a number of things that can be done to form an accurate diagnosis of Parkinson's disease. First, the neurologist needs to collect a history of the illness. Simply listing the symptoms does not guarantee a proper diagnosis, however. A more thorough investigation of the illness is needed.

The following information can help the doctor with the diagnosis:

- The patient's personal and family history; a history of childhood diseases and present medical conditions; medical conditions that have occurred in other family members, such as parents, grandparents, aunts, and uncles; and a history of head or spinal injury.

- What medication the patient is taking, if any (certain drugs can cause PD-like symptoms).

- When illness began, what the symptoms are, and when they occur. Do the symptoms become a problem more when the body is at rest or during activity? Does exercising ease the symptoms? How severe are the symptoms?

- Have the symptoms worsened since they first appeared? How quickly have they progressed?

- Has the patient ever had prolonged exposure to toxic chemicals in the home or at work? If so, to what substances?[4]

Physical Examination

Once the doctor has collected information from the patient, the next step is a physical examination. If the doctor suspects Parkinson's, the patient will be tested for some of the typical PD symptoms. For instance, if the tremors are not obvious during the visit, the doctor may place a sheet of paper over the patient's hands to see if the paper stays still or vibrates somewhat. The doctor may also look at a sample of the patient's handwriting. (PD symptoms may affect handwriting.)

The patient may be asked to walk across the room. The doctor may also move the patient's joints back and forth to check for rigidity. PD patients with symptoms of rigidity cannot make smooth movements. They tend to make short, catching movements. Signs of PD may also include shuffling (walking without lifting one's feet off the floor) or walking on tiptoe.

Bradykinesia (slow movement) may be checked by having the patient perform certain movements or tasks, such as opening and

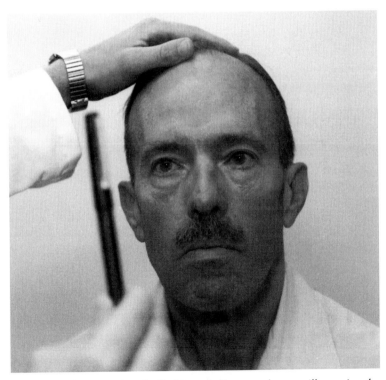

In a physical examination for Parkinson's disease, a doctor will examine the patient to see if there is any sign of limited eye movement.

closing the hands and tapping the fingers and feet. If the movements appear jerky, slow, or erratic, this could be a sign of bradykinesia. The patient may also be asked to put together a puzzle so that the doctor can observe coordination. How a patient gets up from a chair can also be revealing. Many PD patients need to rock back and forth to raise themselves up.

The doctor will also probably examine the patient's eye movements. The patient is asked to move his or her eyes up, down, and side to side. The doctor can then determine if there is any sign of limited eye movement, which is sometimes seen in Parkinson's.[5]

Laboratory Testing

There is no special test that can detect Parkinson's disease. But doctors often perform certain laboratory tests that can rule out other conditions that resemble PD.

A complete physical exam should include blood tests, urine analysis, and cholesterol readings. More extensive testing may include a CAT or CT scan (computerized axial tomogram), which uses tiny streams of X-rays sent through the body at various angles, or MRI (magnetic resonance imaging). Both of these techniques produce revealing pictures of the brain, far clearer and more detailed than the image provided by an ordinary X-ray.

MRI, which was developed after the CAT scan, is more commonly used on PD patients. The patient lays down on a table and is moved into a large machine, which generates a strong magnetic field and sends radio waves through the brain. The radio waves produce characteristic changes in the way the nuclei of certain atoms in the tissues spin, resulting in a pattern of vibration, or resonance. A detector picks up the resonance signals, which are interpreted by a computer to show the density of various parts of the brain tissue in the form of a display on a computer screen. An MRI scan can detect tumors, cysts, abscesses, or other problems that could be harming the nervous system.

Another type of medical imaging is called positron emission tomography, or PET. The PET scanner uses radiations, but instead of beaming them into the patient, it records tiny bursts of radiation coming from inside the patient's body. Before taking a PET scan, the patient is injected with a sugar solution "tagged" with atoms that emit very active particles, called positrons. This solution is absorbed by the body's active brain cells, which give

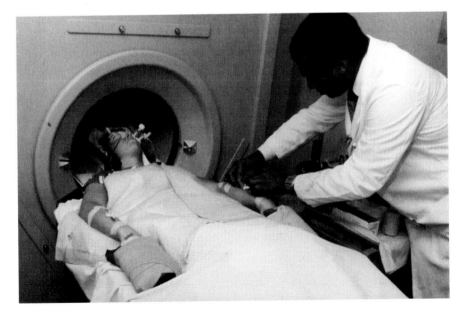

Positron emission tomography (PET) can detect and locate various brain chemicals and provide a picture of the chemical activity in the tissues.

off positrons. (The idea of radioactivity sounds really dangerous, but the amount is actually too small to be harmful.) Special detectors pick up traces of positrons, and these traces are used by a computer to build up the picture in a PET scanner. The PET scan can actually detect and locate various brain chemicals and provide a picture of the chemical activity in the tissues. It might even be able to detect a loss of dopamine before Parkinson's symptoms develop. Unfortunately, PET scanning is very expensive, and it is not widely available.[6]

Researchers have recently developed an even better scanning technique, which can detect Parkinson's disease at an earlier stage. A synthetic compound called altropane, which is chemically similar to cocaine, makes neurons that are transmitting dopamine light up brightly when they are scanned by single photon emission computed tomography. This technique does not involve radioactive compounds and is much cheaper than PET scanning. As PD progresses and dopamine-producing neurons are lost, the scans obtained with altropane become fainter—quite different from the scans from normal brains.[7]

It is important to determine exactly what illness is causing the patient's symptoms because different conditions require different treatments. As with many diseases, it is best to diagnose Parkinson's as soon as possible. A variety of treatments are available that can relieve the symptoms. There are even some medications that may be able to slow the progression of the disease.

6

Treating
Parkinson's Disease

arl Bell, the health editor at *Parade Magazine*, has been an active, energetic person his whole life. Even in his sixties, he still loves to play tennis and go cycling. But Bell first suspected he had Parkinson's disease at age sixty-three, when he noticed that his handwriting looked a little odd as he was writing in his diary. He became especially worried when he got a call from the bank. They questioned him about a $2,000 check that was drawn on his account because the signature did not look like his—it was sloppy and illegible. But Bell knew that he had signed the check. After he noticed a slight tremble in his right hand, he decided to see the doctor. The doctor agreed with Bell's suspicion—it was Parkinson's disease. His doctor referred him to a neurologist. The neurologist confirmed the Parkinson's diagnosis and prescribed medication to alleviate the symptoms.

At sixty-seven, Bell has not allowed his condition to control his life. He continues to take a drug combination of Artane and deprenyl to treat his symptoms. Artane has greatly reduced the tremors in his right hand and deprenyl is supposed to slow down the progression of the disease. Bell also gets plenty of exercise. He still plays tennis and rides his bike to stay in shape. Keeping his muscles strong and flexible has helped him manage his symptoms better. Although Bell still shuffles as he walks, he can move smoothly across a room. Bell is happy that he can still live a normal life—working long hours, climbing stairs, playing tennis, going to the movies, and visiting friends. He types more slowly on his computer and makes more typos than he used to, but he can depend on the computer's spell check to catch most of them. Earl Bell hopes to be still functioning well into his eighties.[1]

Some Parkinson's patients do not respond well to drug treatment, and need to turn to more drastic measures. Terrie Whitling was diagnosed with Parkinson's when she was in her thirties. Her condition became so severe that she says she could not walk more than 30 feet and had to use a wheelchair to get around. She used to love to play tennis, but she had to give it up when the disease took its toll. Unfortunately, Whitling's medication was not doing a good job controlling her symptoms. The drugs did not always work, and when they did, she never knew how effective they would be or for how long. Whitling was the perfect candidate for brain surgery. Brain surgery is a very risky procedure, but fortunately, Whitling was very happy with the results. She felt like she had gotten her life back—she could even play tennis again. "I still take medications. I still have good times and bad. But the good times are 100 percent better than they were ten years ago and the bad times are not a fraction of what they used to be. I felt like I woke up," she says.[2]

At this time, there is no magic pill or procedure that can repair the damaged nerve cells in Parkinson's patients. Treatment basically concentrates on controlling symptoms so that patients can live functional lives.

Drug Therapy

Drug therapy has become an important part of treating Parkinson's disease since the discovery of dopamine's role in PD in the 1960s. When scientists realized that a lack of dopamine caused symptoms to appear, it seemed logical to simply replace the missing dopamine. But patients cannot be treated directly with dopamine because this chemical cannot pass through the blood-brain barrier, a complicated network of tiny blood vessels and cells that screens out many chemicals in the blood and protects the delicate brain cells from their possibly harmful effects. Scientists soon discovered that levodopa, or L-dopa, a related chemical, can pass through the blood-brain barrier. Enzymes in the brain then convert the levodopa to dopamine. Levodopa does not stop the progress of the disease, but it does relieve the symptoms, and it brings a more normal life to many people who were helpless and confined to wheelchairs. Unfortunately, levodopa can have a number of unwanted side effects, including nausea, vomiting, low blood pressure, restlessness, and a kind of twitching in the limbs called dyskinesia. Dyskinesia is a side effect commonly seen in PD patients who are taking too much levodopa. Doses of the drug must be adjusted carefully for each individual patient. Side effects are more likely to occur in people who take large doses for a long period of time.

There are some additional problems in long-term levodopa treatment. Many patients get a "wearing-off effect," in which symptoms worsen before the next scheduled dose. The problem is that the drug gradually loses its effectiveness. As a result, the dosage needs to be increased to achieve the same effectiveness, which may cause more side effects.

The "on/off effect" is another problem that occurs in about 30 to 40 percent of PD patients. When this happens, the patient may suddenly "freeze" and become unable to move for a few seconds or even a few minutes. These episodes may occur several times a day, and they can be very frightening to patients. But there are little "tricks" that patients can use to help them to somehow move across the room even if they cannot walk.[3]

Levodopa is often used in combination with a drug called carbidopa to increase the treatment's effectiveness. Carbidopa stops an enzyme from destroying large amounts of levodopa before it reaches the brain. This allows more levodopa to get to the brain. Sinemet (the brand name for a combination of carbidopa and levodopa) contains a smaller dose of levodopa, which helps to reduce some of the side effects. Although Sinemet greatly reduces PD symptoms, especially bradykinesia and rigidity, it does not get rid of all symptoms.[4]

In the late 1970s, Walter Birkmayer (who was the first to use levodopa) discovered that the drug deprenyl might actually slow the progression of Parkinson's disease. In 1983, after analyzing a study of 323 patients who were treated with levodopa and deprenyl for two to eight years, Dr. Birkmayer found that these patients lived longer than 285 patients treated with levodopa without deprenyl did. Birkmayer's discovery did not receive any attention, however, until it was found that MPTP can cause PD.

Tricking the Brain

Tom Riess, a man diagnosed with Parkinson's sixteen years ago at the age of thirty-three, found a way to help PD patients move even when they are unable to walk. Using visual cues, such as spacing pennies along the floor, Riess found that by concentrating visually on these objects, he could move himself even when he was in a "frozen" state.

In 1993, Riess got an idea when he heard about a virtual reality-type headgear developed by a company called Virtual Vision. He thought about developing a virtual reality (VR) device that incorporated visual cues than could help PD patients who frequently freeze and cannot move. Riess contacted the company and soon teamed up with the company's director of interface design, Suzanne Weghorst, who was also a psychologist. Together they developed a special device that includes a tinted sports visor with a liquid crystal display mounted above one eye. A reflecting lens attached to the visor below the line of vision projects the image on the display back into the eye. The image appears closer than it actually is.

In 1996, Reiss and Weghorst published preliminary results of a study on twenty PD patients. The "virtual cues" provided by the device helped these patients to walk and even run during freezing episodes. The visor can be worn like sunglasses, so it is easier to handle than the typical VR head-mounted gear. The device has some disadvantages, though—the patient needs to carry around a video player and other equipment to get a good video signal. This may make it difficult for the average PD patient to use. In addition, people may not like wearing the device out in public. Reiss believes the concept of tricking the brain with visual cues is an important discovery and hopes that perhaps one day a tiny implant in the retina or the brain could be used to provide the visual cues.[5]

Deprenyl is often used along with levodopa to control PD symptoms. Some doctors believe that deprenyl should be the first drug to be used by PD patients to slow the progression of the disease. Further studies conducted in 1989 showed that newly diagnosed PD patients could be helped for about a year by deprenyl alone, before it was necessary to add levodopa. Researchers concluded that deprenyl served as a kind of protection, and slowed down the damage to the brain cells.[6] Some health experts are not convinced about the benefits of deprenyl, however, and its use remains controversial.

Another type of antiparkinson drug belongs to a class called anticholinergic drugs. Remember that the neurotransmitter acetylcholine depends on a regular supply of dopamine for smooth muscle movement. When dopamine is depleted, however, acetylcholine continues to flow, causing an imbalance of the neurotransmitters. Anticholinergic drugs reduce symptoms by blocking the action of acetylcholine. Health experts say that only

A Drug to Eat

Australian researchers report that broad beans *(Vicia faba)* provide a natural source of levodopa. A 3.5-ounce (100 grams) serving of this vegetable contains about 250 milligrams of levodopa. People with Parkinson's disease normally take from 300 to 2,500 milligrams of levodopa, so the dose of the drug has to be adjusted if broad beans are eaten regularly. The broad beans should be eaten whole, since the pods contain most of the levodopa. They are effective even after freezing or canning and cooking.[7]

about 50 percent of people respond to the anticholinergic drugs, however. In addition, these drugs do not usually work for patients with severe PD symptoms.

Dopamine agonists are drugs that work by stimulating dopamine receptors in the basal ganglia, thus mimicking the effects of dopamine. These drugs can be used alone or in combination with levodopa. They permit a 5–30 percent reduction in the dosage of levodopa. Dopamine agonists are most effective during the early stages of PD.[8] Recent studies suggest that it might be advisable to start with dopamine agonists, and then use levodopa as a second-step supplement when the treatment becomes less effective. Patients taking the dopamine agonist ropinirole have good control of symptoms, and less dyskinesia. After a five-year study, only 20 percent of patients taking ropinirole had dyskinesia, compared to 45 percent in a group of PD patients receiving levodopa. By this time, two-thirds of the ropinirole patients were taking levodopa to keep severe PD symptoms in check.[9]

Studies of what happens chemically to dopamine and levodopa in the body have recently led to the development of a whole new class of PD drugs. One of the reasons levodopa eventually loses its effectiveness is that it is broken down into various ineffective products before it can reach the brain. The drug carbidopa is used to prevent one type of enzymatic breakdown, but it cannot prevent the action of a different enzyme, catechol-O-methyltransferase (COMT). This enzyme converts levodopa to a form that is not only useless in restoring dopamine levels but may compete with levodopa for transport into the brain. COMT inhibitors block the action of this enzyme. Recently developed drugs of this group, such as entacapone, keep the levodopa concentration in the blood at an effective level longer and help to keep the level more stable. Researchers believe that this may also help to prevent some of the negative side effects of levodopa, such as dyskinesias, which are observed when the levodopa levels rise or fall sharply.[10]

Patients are often given a combination of different antiparkinson drugs to increase the effectiveness of the treatment. The treatment is lifelong, and it is likely that the dosage will need to be adjusted as the disease progresses over the years.

Drugs Used to Treat Parkinson's Disease

Dopamine suppliers:	levodopa (L-dopa)
Enzyme inhibitors:	carbidopa, deprenyl (selegiline and Eldepryl)
COMT inhibitors:	entacapone, tolcapone
Anticholinergic drugs:	Artane, Akineton, Cogentin, Kemadrin
Dopamine agonists:	bromocriptine (Parlodel), pergolide (Permax), pramipexole (Mirapex), and ropinirole (Requip)
Antiviral drugs:	amantadine (Symmetrel)

Surgical Treatments

Brain surgery used to be a common practice for treating PD symptoms. Surgery generally involved destroying nerve cells in a tiny part of the brain to relieve severe PD symptoms, such as uncontrollable tremors. By the 1960s, when antiparkinson drugs became widely available, surgical treatments lost their popularity. But with major medical advances over the years, brain surgery is once again becoming an option for PD patients, especially for those with severe symptoms that cannot be helped by drugs.

Pallidotomy is a surgical procedure that has been around since the late 1930s. In this operation, the surgeon targets a tiny group of nerve fibers in a structure called the globus pallidus, found in the basal ganglia. The globus pallidus contains nerve cells that transmit messages for movement. In Parkinson's disease, the globus pallidus becomes overactive, causing an overflow of messages. As a result, PD symptoms develop, such as tremors, rigidity, slowness of movement, and freezing. Doctors can alleviate most of these symptoms by destroying the nerve cells in the globus pallidus.

During a pallidotomy, the neurosurgeon uses modern imaging techniques to zero in on the target area. Then, after drilling a hole in the skull, the surgeon inserts an electrode that produces electricity and heat to destroy small amounts of brain tissue in the globus pallidus. The patient is awake under local anesthesia during the operation so that the doctor can ask the patient questions to check on improvement of the symptoms. If the pallidotomy is successful, the results are often dramatic: PD symptoms disappear right away, and patients who were once wheelchair-bound can walk again. Doctors are not sure, however, what the long-lasting effects will be.[11]

Thalamotomy is another kind of surgical procedure available to PD patients. It had replaced pallidotomy in the 1950s as techniques became more advanced. During a thalamotomy, the surgeon destroys a tiny group of cells in the thalamus, a message-relay station in the mid-brain. The procedure is performed on just one side of the brain, which relieves severe tremors on the opposite side of the body. Unfortunately, it is too risky to work on

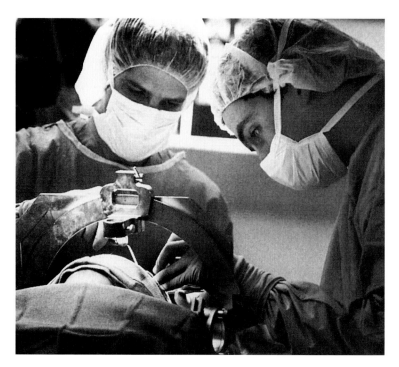

Pallidotomy is a procedure in which the surgeon inserts an electrode into the patient's nerve fibers in the brain. The electrode produces electricity and heat to destroy small amounts of brain tissue, alleviating PD symptoms such as tremors, rigidity, slowness of movement, and freezing.

both sides of the brain because of the danger of severe side effects.[12]

Although pallidotomy and thalamotomy are much safer and more effective than they were years ago, they still involve a serious risk and can result in complications. Pallidotomy may cause such problems as confusion, sleepiness, speech problems, weakness of arm and leg muscles, balance problems, and vision problems. Thalamotomy may cause such problems as seizures, walking and balance problems, speech difficulties, and memory problems. These procedures should be done by an experienced neurosurgeon to minimize the risk. Doctors do not recommend brain surgery for all PD patients. Patients who have severe PD symptoms and no longer respond to drug therapy are candidates for such a procedure.[13] Younger patients seem to respond better to surgical treatment.

Surgical procedures do not eliminate the need for antiparkinson drugs. The patient must continue to take medication to relieve the remaining symptoms.

Deep brain stimulation (or DBS) is a procedure that is far less risky than other surgical procedures because no brain tissue is destroyed. Instead, a high-frequency electric current is used to paralyze the overactive brain cells that cause tremors. A small pacemaker-like pulse generator is surgically inserted near the patient's collarbone. It is connected to an electrode implanted in the thalamus. The generator sends out electric pulses to the thalamus that the patient can turn on and off by placing a magnet over the skin. When the device is on, it stops the tremors. The generator needs to be replaced every three to five years. The procedure is effective in many cases, but it is rather costly— around $20,000. Moreover, it only helps to relieve tremors, but does not usually relieve other PD symptoms, such as rigidity and bradykinesia.

Researchers are also investigating pulse generators implanted in other parts of the brain, including the globus pallidus and the subthalamic nucleus, which are involved in symptoms of rigidity and involuntary motion. Deep brain stimulation in the subthalamic nucleus, for instance, has shown great promise. Nicole Stedman, a sixty-one-year-old California woman, turned to DBS because the drugs used to treat her Parkinson's condition were making her feel worse instead of better. Electrodes were implanted in both sides of Stedman's subthalamic nucleus. The results were remarkable. Her violent tremors were gone, and she felt like a new person. She still needed medication, but the dose was cut down significantly, to only a fraction of her usual dose.[14]

Eat a Good Diet

Health experts agree that people should eat a well balanced diet in order to stay healthy. Eating a wide variety of foods can help a person's body stay strong so that it can defend itself against illness and injury. This is especially important for people who are battling a sickness, including Parkinson's disease.

There is some controversial evidence that vitamin C and vitamin E, which are found in foods, can help reduce PD symptoms and even slow the progression of the disease. Studies have shown that vitamin C and vitamin E protect body chemicals from oxidative reactions and the potentially harmful free radicals they generate. Remember that the free radicals can cause damage to the nerve cells, including those in the substantial nigra. Researchers continue to study these vitamins to determine if they are an effective treatment for Parkinson's disease.[15]

Diet is also important because it could interfere with the absorption of medication. For instance, some PD patients who take levodopa should also stay away from a high-protein diet. Certain amino acids may block levodopa from getting to the brain, which reduces the effectiveness of the drug.[16] Protein should not be eliminated from the diet, but it should fall in the range of 30 to 50 grams a day, which is the U.S. Recommended Daily Allowance.[17]

Exercise

Exercise is very important for Parkinson's patients, especially because their movements are affected. Exercise will not keep the disease from getting worse, but it may help strengthen the muscles so the patient can move around better. Muscles usually work better the more we use them, as long as we don't overdo it. Exercise may include walking, jogging, participating in sports, or swimming—as long as the body is moving and working the muscles. Stretching is also important. Stretching the muscles makes them more flexible, and reduces muscle rigidity.

Exercise can bring a wide range of benefits to Parkinson's patients. Patients with rigid muscles can gain better mobility with muscle-strengthening exercises and keep their muscle tone. Exercise can also help improve balance, posture, and walking problems, and can even strengthen the muscles used for speaking and swallowing. Exercise can also help the patient feel better emotionally. Depression is often associated with Parkinson's.

They've Got Rhythm

Research at Colorado State University has shown that music can help in rehabilitating Parkinson's patients. The musical rhythms produce a response in the patients' brains and help to stimulate walking movements. The scientists are using PET scanners to study how the brain perceives and produces rhythm and integrates it with movement. Learning the scientific basis of music therapy, they say, will help in getting more coverage of the therapy by medical insurance—an important consideration for PD patients.[18]

Exercise can create a feeling of accomplishment and give the patient a feeling of control. In addition, rigorous exercise triggers "feel-good" chemicals, called endorphins, which are released in the body. Joggers often experience a "runner's high," because of a rush of endorphins. Exercise can also relieve stress, which is often a factor in triggering PD symptoms.[19]

7

Parkinson's Disease and Society

Parkinson's disease has received a lot of extra publicity since Michael J. Fox revealed his condition in 1998. But many people had been working hard in the fight against Parkinson's disease for years before Fox decided to devote his time and efforts to increasing public awareness and raising funds for Parkinson's research. In 1991, two Parkinson's patients, Michel Monnot and Ava Crowder, went on a fundraising tour from Miami to Maine. Although Monnot and Crowder were disabled in some ways, they still managed to walk about five miles each day as Crowder's husband drove them around and dropped them off from city to city. They were able to walk thanks to a regimen of deprenyl with levodopa, diet, and exercise.

Monnot and Crowder were on a mission. They wanted to raise money for more effective Parkinson's drugs and to increase public awareness about this mysterious disease. At each stop, they urged people with Parkinson's disease to "come out of the closet" and show other people that Parkinson's patients can function normally in society. People tend to judge people with PD unfairly. "Lots of times, we're mistaken for drunks," Monnot said. "Balance is difficult to keep." Monnot had also been embarrassed to eat in public. Before his medication kicked in, he would often drop his food and drool.[1]

Attitudes About Parkinson's

Unfortunately, people sometimes view Parkinson's symptoms—including severe shaking, slow movement, rigidity, and speech problems—as signs of senility. The truth is, people with PD are quite competent. They may have lost part of their brain, but not their mind. Fearing negative reactions, however, many Parkinson's patients find it pretty scary to go out in public when a hand may start shaking uncontrollably or a leg suddenly becomes stiff. They may try to hide their symptoms by putting their hands in their pockets or using some other little trick to conceal their condition.

Michael J. Fox kept his condition a secret for seven years. He had to spend a lot of time and energy trying to hide his symptoms. Millions of people were watching his every move. (Remember how anxious he was sitting in his limousine outside the Golden Globe Awards, waiting for his drugs to take effect as his arm and leg were shaking uncontrollably.) Fox also told *People Magazine* that he had a close call one time at the David Letterman show. While waiting backstage, Fox's arms were shaking uncontrollably. He remembers just praying that the medication would kick in before he was introduced. By the time he went out for his interview with Letterman, Fox's symptoms were gone, and no one was the wiser.[2] Now that Michael J. Fox has opened up to the public about his condition, he says that he feels like a heavy load has been lifted. In fact, he has become very open about his condition, even when his symptoms become obvious. For instance, Fox came in late to an interview with a *Newsweek* reporter, and he was walking with a bowlegged shuffle. "I'm just waiting for the pill to kick in," he said casually, and asked if they could wait for a few minutes so he could settle down.[3]

Former Attorney General Janet Reno, on the other hand, in her usual straightforward manner, told the public about her Parkinson's condition as soon as she received her diagnosis. And unlike most Parkinson's patients, Reno does not worry about what people think when they see her shaking uncontrollably. She has made no efforts to hide her condition. As Attorney General, she was more concerned about fulfilling the duties of her job. Reno understands that she is a role model for many Parkinson's patients, but she has decided not to participate in a crusade against PD. She has, for the most part, dealt with her condition in a private manner. At the end of her eight years as Attorney General, Reno briefly retired to private life but still remained active, driving cross-country and going on extended kayaking trips. In September 2001, she plunged back into politics and became a candidate for Governor of her home state, Florida. Opponents and reporters brought up her Parkinson's disease, especially the possibility that she might develop dementia. Reno said she had been cleared by her doctors and declared, "I think I can do it, otherwise I wouldn't be here."[4] She told reporters, "You all just have to get used to the shaking."[5]

Michael J. Fox and Janet Reno have made an important

impact on people's attitudes toward Parkinson's patients. They are living proof that people with Parkinson's can function normally in society. With such prominent examples, attitudes are slowly changing as more people open their eyes to the truth about Parkinson's disease.

Risky Business

Many people would agree that Muhammad Ali brought class to the world of boxing. The self-proclaimed "Greatest of All Time," Ali was considered a hero to millions. At the height of his boxing career, he amazed fans with his remarkable speed and grace in the ring. Ali was arrogant yet charming at the same time. This strong, skillful boxer was also a poet, and he would speak in poetic rhymes to describe how he would defeat his opponents. So when Ali revealed that he had parkinsonism, people all over the world were shocked and saddened.

The revelation of Muhammad Ali's condition also added new fuel to an ongoing controversy about the dangers of boxing. In 1984, the American Medical Association (AMA) recommended that boxing should be banned. They argued that boxing is a brutal sport, in which its main objective is to injure the opponent and produce brain trauma serious enough to cause unconsciousness. This is not the case in other sports; head injuries to football and hockey players, for example, are accidental and not intentional. There are serious safety issues in boxing, including the fact that professional boxers do not wear headgear to protect themselves from head injury. Dr. George Lundberg, editor of the *Journal of the American Medical Association* (JAMA) argued during a debate that permanent brain damage is more commonly seen in boxers than in the rest of the population. In addition, some medical experts believe that such brain damage can increase the risk for developing Parkinson's disease or Alzheimer's disease.

Boxing supporters concede that there are some problems with the sport, but they believe that banning boxing is not the answer. Larry Hazzard, Sr., commissioner of the New Jersey Athletic Control Board (the state agency that oversees boxing), says that there is a basic need in a certain part of society to watch people engage in physical combat, and it brings the viewers enjoyment. He believes that boxing gives people an outlet for their aggression in a safe and regulated form. Dr. Barry Jordan, medical director of the New York State Athletic Commission, which governs boxing in that state, argues that banning boxing would only force the sport to go underground, without any regulation, which would be much more dangerous. Instead, Dr. Jordan suggested that additional safety measures should be implemented, and existing rules should be enforced. For instance, a fighter who is suspended would not be allowed to fight in another state before his injuries are healed. Dr. Jordan also supported the suggestion that boxers go through a medical exam, including a CT scan, before a fight. Dr. Lundberg, however, notes that a pre-fight exam is not realistic because it would be too costly.

Boxing trainer Teddy Atlas, who worked with heavyweight champions Mike Tyson and Michael Moorer, said that boxing has a much lower rate of injury than football. He pointed out that when football players get injured, they are back on the playing field a week later. If a boxer is knocked out, however, he is suspended for ninety days and can fight again only if he passes a CT scan. Atlas also believes that efforts are better spent on

Helpful Dogs

Companion animals can provide a great deal of emotional support to people with chronic health problems such as Parkinson's disease, and they can also provide some practical help. Dogs have been trained to turn on light switches, open doors, pull wheelchairs, pick up fallen objects, and do other tasks to make the disabled more independent.

Lou Paulmier, a Parkinson's patient for almost thirty years, had settled into a very quiet, sedentary lifestyle. He not only had tremors and stiffness, but he also experienced "freezing" episodes. A specially trained dog named Melek, which means "Angel" in Turkish, turned Paulmier into a more active person in just a matter of weeks. When Lou freezes, he gives Melek a sign. Melek nudges Paulmier's foot with his paw, and somehow Paulmier manages to move. If he does fall, Melek helps him get up.[6]

Peter Morabito, a Parkinson's patient, tends to fall a lot because his severe tremors make him lose his balance. One of his many falls resulted in a fractured hip that he had to have repaired surgically. He even wore shoulder pads and knee pads to protect him from injury. Then a Great Dane called Victor came to the rescue. Victor was trained to handle patients like Morabito. He learned to detect when Morabito was having a problem. The dog would adjust his position while Morabito was walking to help him to keep his balance. When Morabito did fall, Victor would come next to him, and Morabito would say "brace." Victor would straighten his legs, and Morabito would use him as a support to climb up. Peter Morabito used to fall forty to fifty times a day. Now he falls only three to four times a day.[7]

Melek, right, places her paw on Louis Paulmier's foot to remind him to regain his balance during a walk. Paulmier, who has Parkinson's disease, is among a small group in a program pairing Parkinson's sufferers with well-trained dogs.

making boxing safer rather than banning the sport altogether, which could create a major upset in society.[8]

Living With Parkinson's

Parkinson's disease has an enormous impact on the lifestyle and quality of life, not only of people who have it, but also on their family and other caregivers. As the disease progresses, a person needs increasing help with many daily activities, including dressing, making and eating meals, and going to the bathroom. According to the National Family Caregivers Association (NFCA), only 20 percent of Americans who need long-term care receive it in institutions; in many cases, the care is provided by family members.[9]

The caregivers carry a tremendous, ongoing burden that may consume many hours a week. In a 1997 NFCA survey, caregivers said they experienced emotions including frustration, anxiety, compassion, and sadness. They suffered from a sense of isolation and a loss of personal and leisure time. They developed problems from back pains and headaches to sleeplessness, stomach disorders, and depression. And yet, more than two-thirds said they "found an inner strength I didn't know I had," and more than one-third said they developed a closer relationship with the person for whom they were caring.[10]

8

Parkinson's Disease and the Future

In July 1997, fifty-three-year-old Steve Ashworth, who had suffered the debilitating effects of Parkinson's disease for fourteen years, was filled with hope when he signed up to participate in the first government-financed study of fetal-cell transplants. Fetal-cell transplantation involves taking cells from the brains of aborted fetuses and implanting them into the brain of a Parkinson's patient. Scientists hoped that these implanted cells would survive in their new home and produce dopamine to restore the brain's dopamine deficiency.

Ashworth was one of forty Parkinson's patients who would undergo an operation in a four-year study headed by Dr. Curt Freed, a neurologist at the University of Colorado. The participants were informed that they would be randomly assigned to one of two groups. But they did not know in which group they would be placed. Subjects belonging to the first group, called the treatment group, were implanted with brain tissue from four

Embryonic stem cells can mature into any cell or tissue, and scientists such as Dr. Tom Okarma, president and CEO of Geron Corporation, the company where stem cell research is performed, say that they may someday be used to repair or replace damaged tissue due to Parkinson's disease.

aborted fetuses. Individuals in the second group, called the placebo control group, had a "sham" operation. These patients did not receive any fetal tissue.

All the participants underwent an operation that involved drilling four holes into the skull. The patients were sedated but awake during the operation. For those in the treatment group, the surgeons injected two droplets of fetal tissue, containing about two million dopamine-producing cells, into the putamen, a structure in the brain that controls movement. Dr. Freed hoped that at least 100,000 cells would survive and take hold. The patients in the control group were not implanted with fetal tissue, but the surgeons made the operations appear the same so that the participants did not know whether they received the real treatment or not. Having a control group is especially important since many Parkinson's patients experience a "placebo effect," in which an ineffective substitute for a drug or surgical procedure seems to produce a positive effect because the subjects believe they have received the real treatment. Critics say that the sham operation is not a good control for the placebo effect because unlike other experiments, which use a simple sugar pill, performing an actual operation involves some risk. Dr. Freed says the risk of the fake surgery is "similar to the risk of going to the dentist."[1] According to the researchers, having a control group to determine the placebo effect is essential to show whether the treatment is really effective.

Thirteen months after his surgery, Steve Ashworth finally found out that his surgery was a fake. Ashworth's hopes for a quick recovery were dashed, but as a participant in the control group, he was offered the real thing. Fourteen of the twenty placebo patients had already chosen to get the real surgery even though the results of the study had not come in yet. Ashworth was unsure about the risks and decided to delay his choice until he found out the results of the experiment, which were finally announced in April 1999.[2]

The findings were not as dramatic as the researchers had hoped. The surgery itself went well. Imaging tests showed that the transplanted cells survived in sixteen out of nineteen recipients who completed the study. However, there seemed to be significant improvement only in patients younger than sixty. For some reason, the results for the older subjects varied greatly:

Some improved somewhat, but others got even worse. On the average, patients older than sixty did not show any real improvement. In addition, in neither age group did the surgery help ease the tremors that are a common symptom of Parkinson's. It did relieve symptoms of rigidity and slowness of movement, however.[3]

Researchers explain that this surgery is still in an experimental stage and gives important clues for further research. Dr. Freed is working to improve the surgical technique and advises his patients to put off the surgery as long as possible.[4]

Fetal-Cell Research

Researchers have been exploring fetal-cell research since the 1980s. In the early 1980s, Dr. Freed was already convinced that drugs were not the answer to PD and was attempting to develop a kind of cell therapy that would replace the missing dopamine. In experiments on rats, he learned that if nerve cells are taken from an embryo and implanted into the brain, the cells can survive. The implanted cells would then make connections with other nerve cells, and could repair or replace damaged nerve tissues. The next step would be to apply this finding to humans, by taking brain cells from aborted fetuses and implanting them into a human patient's brain.[5] Cells from fetal tissue are suitable for this treatment because they grow much faster than the tissue of adults. Fetal tissue taken at an early stage of development also does not have a developed immune system and therefore, it is less likely to be rejected by a recipient's body.[6]

By 1988, Dr. Freed was ready to perform the operation on people.[7] Unfortunately, fetal tissue research was and still is very controversial. Activists who believe that life begins at conception argue that it is unethical to use aborted fetuses in medical research. They fear that giving pregnant women the option to donate fetal tissue for medical purposes would encourage abortion. Researchers counter that other motivations are far more important in a woman's decision whether or not to have an abortion.

An advisory committee from the National Institutes of Health looked into the matter and concluded that the procedure was not unethical and showed great promise for future research.[8] Unfortunately, in March 1988, the Reagan Administration ignored these findings and banned federal funding for any medical research that involved fetal tissue. By November, on the same day that George Bush was elected president, Dr. Freed used private funds to perform the first fetal-cell transplant in the United States.

The recipient was Don Nelson, a patient who had been battling Parkinson's for twenty years. Don was very pleased with the results. The procedure changed his life. Don is still doing well over a decade later, although he had to have a second operation because the implanted cells from the first one had died. Now in his sixties, Don is strong enough to help his son build a house. He used to have trouble picking up small objects, but now he has no problem holding onto screws and nails.[9]

The ban on federal funding for fetal-cell research continued through the Bush Administration. But Dr. Freed, as well as other researchers, continued their work using private funds. In 1992, the ban was finally lifted by the Clinton Administration. At that time, Dr. Freed teamed up with neurologist Stanley Fahn from Columbia Presbyterian Center in Manhattan, and together they devised a plan for what later became the first federally funded fetal-cell transplant study.[10]

Since the late 1980s, about 250 fetal-cell transplants have been performed on Parkinson's patients. And even though the results of the first federally funded study were not very encouraging, there have been a number of amazing success stories like Don Nelson. In 1994, for instance, Dan Stewart, a Parkinson's patient, decided to get a fetal-cell transplant because drugs were no longer helping to relieve his symptoms. The surgery was successful and the cells survived. After sixteen months, Dan was able to stop taking all of his medication. Six years later, he was still drug-free, with only minor Parkinson's symptoms. The procedure is not consistently successful, however. While some people have been helped by these transplants, others have not. Scientists admit there is still a lot to learn.[11]

Fetal-cell transplantation may not become widely available because the supply of fetal tissue is limited. Treating just one Parkinson's patient requires tissue from four or more aborted fetuses. Therefore, scientists are looking into alternative sources of cells, including xenotransplantation—transplanting cells from other species.[12] Researchers have been working with fetal brain cells from pigs. Although monkeys are considered to be our closest relatives, pigs are good candidates for xenotransplants because they are widely available and their organs and body chemistry are similar to ours. Using brain tissue from pigs instead of humans is less controversial, but it does spark some concerns about the animal tissue transmitting diseases. To minimize the health risks, the pigs are raised in a controlled environment, and screened for bacteria and viruses.[13]

A study on pig-cell transplants was conducted in 1995 and 1996 by a team of researchers at the Boston Medical Center/Boston University School of Medicine. Scientists performed twelve pig-cell transplants on patients with advanced Parkinson's disease. Each patient was implanted with twelve million fetal pig cells into three different areas of the brain. In any transplant, whether it involves human or animal tissue, there is a risk for immune rejection. That means that the patient's immune system may recognize the transplanted tissue as foreign and attack it. Therefore, half of the patients were given immunosuppressant drugs to prevent rejection, and the other half received cells that had been treated with an antibody that lowered the chances of rejection. Both groups did well after the procedure, and showed no signs of rejection.[14]

The results of the pig-cell transplant study were reported in the March 14, 2000 issue of *Neurology*, the American Academy of Neurology's scientific journal. On the average, there was a 19 percent improvement of symptoms among the subjects within a year after surgery. But some people showed little improvement, and some even had slightly worse symptoms. Yet three of the patients had improved 34–51 percent. One man who before the transplant needed a cane to walk and sometimes had to crawl up a flight of stairs, could now walk easily without a cane for much of the day. He also could do more tasks with his hands, and he did not even need to take his medication at certain times of the day. Interestingly, brain scans did not show any increase in the level of dopamine even in the people that showed significant improvement. Researchers theorized that in these patients, the cells that survived produced enough dopamine to relieve symptoms, but not enough to show up on the scans.[15]

Genetically Altered Animals

It was a medical miracle in 1997 when scientists first cloned a sheep, which they named Dolly, using cells taken from an adult sheep. Three years later, the same group that cloned Dolly cloned five pigs from the cells of an adult sow, using a more advanced technique than the one used to create Dolly.

Scientists hope that these pigs can provide a supply of organs, cells, or tissues to be used in xenotransplants. Because rejection is a major concern in xenotransplants, scientists would like to genetically engineer these pigs to avoid this problem. For instance, scientists hope to "knock out" the gene for an enzyme that puts certain sugar molecules on pig cells that would be recognized as foreign by the human body, causing the person's immune system to attack the pig cells and reject the transplant. By deactivating this gene, rejection could be avoided. Scientists would then have to insert three new genes into the pig cells, which is then given to the patient through a blood transfusion about the same time as the transplant.

Company officials have announced their achievement in a scientific journal in the hope of attracting investors. They hope that transplants using genetically altered pig tissue can be tested on humans in a few years. This advance could be very encouraging for the thousands of people who have to wait for organ transplants every year because of a limited supply.

On March 5, 2000, a litter of pigs—Millie, Christa, Alexis, Carrel, and Dotcom—was produced by cloning.

Although the improvement varied from patient to patient, the results were comparable to the first human fetal-cell transplants. A larger study is now underway, involving eighteen patients who will receive four times as many fetal pig brain cells.[16]

Stem-Cell Research

Scientists have made exciting progress in promising new research, which may help in the treatment of a number of conditions, including Parkinson's disease, Alzheimer's disease, and even spinal cord injury.

99

Until the late 1990s, scientists were convinced that if nerve cells in the brain and spinal cord were damaged, they could not grow back, or regenerate, and no new ones were formed after infancy. As more was learned about the nervous system, however, it was discovered that by changing the conditions in the body, this kind of regeneration could be made to take place.

Each body cell is bathed in a fluid that contains a diverse mixture of chemicals, from simple salts to proteins and other complex biochemicals. Some are always present; others are produced in response to an event such as cell damage due to an injury or illness. When a nerve cell is injured, connections between axons and dendrites, linking it to other nerve cells, are broken. The damaged nerve cell attempts to regenerate its missing parts and reestablish the connections. The sensory and motor nerves can do this fairly well, stimulated by body chemicals called nerve growth factors. In the brain and spinal cord, however, there are also various inhibitory chemicals, which prevent regrowth.

Researchers have found that in mammals and other higher animals, the ability for regeneration decreases with age. Early embryos can regenerate virtually anything—that is how identical twins are formed. If cells, known as stem cells, in a very early embryo are separated, each one has the potential to produce all the tissues and organs needed for a fully independent individual. For instance, a stem cell has the potential to grow into any tissue or organ such as a kidney, heart muscle, or brain tissue. Studies on animals such as rats and cats have demonstrated that when stem cells taken from embryos are transplanted into the site of the damage, they can grow in spite of the inhibitory chemicals and restore the broken connections to motor nerves.[17]

Stem-cell research has stirred up controversy much like the one surrounding fetal-cell transplants. Antiabortion activists have spoken out strongly against conducting such research on humans. In 1996, a ban was imposed on government-funded research in the United States involving human embryos, forcing researchers to seek private funding. Supporters of stem-cell research argue that an ample supply of stem cells is available from spontaneous abortions and from the thousands of surplus embryos that are created each year in in-vitro fertilization clinics. (Typically, many more embryos are produced in the artificial fertilization procedure than are actually implanted in the prospective mother. The extra embryos are frozen and may be discarded after a successful pregnancy has occurred.) In fact, not only could the stem cells themselves be used, but they can be grown in cultures, so that huge amounts could be obtained from a few embryonic cells.[18]

Researchers take the cells from an early-stage embryo, less than a week old, before it has had a chance to form any specific functions. The cells are mixed with growth factors to help them grow and multiply. When the growth factors are removed, the stem cells can develop into certain kinds of cells. Suitable treatment, for example, can produce neural stem cells, which can develop into various kinds of nervous-system cells. Scientists are still learning how to control the process to produce whatever kinds of cells they want, but they are making considerable progress. When researchers implanted heart muscle cells grown from mouse stem cells into the hearts of mice, the cells grew successfully and incorporated themselves among the other cells. Dr. Ronald McKay, a research scientist and his colleagues at the National Institute of Neurological Disorders and Stroke

(NINDS), transplanted neural stem cells from rat embryos into the brains of rats with Parkinson's-like symptoms. After eighty days, the rats showed a 75 percent improvement in motor function. Meanwhile, various research teams have been able to grow human heart cells and nerve cells from stem cells. These findings are encouraging, but there is still a lot to learn about stem cells. Human trials may not begin for another few years.[19]

In April 2000, "Superman" Christopher Reeve, who was paralyzed in a horse riding accident in 1995, urged Congress to lift the ban on research involving human embryos. During a Senate subcommittee hearing on a new law proposed to permit federal funding of stem cell research, Mr. Reeve asked, "Is it more ethical for a woman to donate unused embryos that will never become human beings or to let them be tossed away as so much garbage when they could help save thousands of lives?"[20] Critics, on the other hand, contend that destroying human embryos, for any reason, is immoral. In 2001, President George W. Bush announced that federal funding for stem-cell research would be limited to the sixty embryo cell lines that had already been isolated, and a President's Council on Bioethics would be created to oversee such work.[21] With or without federal funding, stem cell research will continue. Unfortunately, as long as this research is in the hands of private companies, the public may not know what kind of progress is being made.[22]

Some researchers believe such a controversy could be avoided if they concentrate their efforts on studying adult stems cells. Adults, too, have stem cells, but just in certain types of tissue. For example, adult stem cells are found in bone marrow, the spongy material inside large bones, where the body's blood cells are produced. Blood cells are constantly wearing out and are replaced by new ones grown from stem cells in the bone marrow.

There are limitations to what adult stem cells can become, however. For instance, stem cells in bone marrow usually develop into different types of blood cells; and stem cells in muscles tend to form new muscle cells. Embryonic cells, on the other hand, can become any kind of tissue in the body, from skin to muscles to neurons. This makes adult stem research a bit trickier to pursue. Some amazing progress has been made, however. Scientists used to think that adult stem cells were not present in the nervous system. In recent experiments, however, neural stem cells have been isolated from the nervous systems of rats and mice. But locating neural stem cells in adult humans may be more complicated. Researchers have isolated what they think may be neural stem cells from brain tissue removed surgically during the treatment of a patient with epilepsy.

The next step was to see if researchers could direct the specialization of adult stem cells. In animal experiments, adult stem cells were taken from the brains of rats and placed into the bone marrow. Surprisingly, the neural cells produced various kinds of blood cells. Even though they didn't form all the blood-cell types, the results were promising because before, scientists did not think that adult stem cells could adapt to a new environment at all. Additional studies with rats showed that stem cells from the bone marrow could produce liver cells. These findings demonstrated that under certain conditions, adult stem cells are more flexible than scientists originally thought.

There is still a lot to learn about adult stem cells in humans. So far, scientists have isolated adult stem cells only in certain types of cells and tissues. They hope eventually to develop techniques to obtain stem cells from a patient with Parkinson's disease or some other brain condition, direct the stem cells to produce nerve tissue in the laboratory, and then implant the new tissue in the patient's brain. If this can be done, there will be very little, if any, risk for rejection.[23]

There are many difficulties, however. Very few adult stem cells are present, and they are often hard to isolate and purify. There might not be time to grow enough in cultures—especially since adult stem cells may not multiply as readily as embryonic or fetal stem cells. And in the case of hereditary disorders, the patient's stem cells would carry the same genetic defect. The genes in adult stem cells might also have been damaged by radiation, chemicals, or other influences over the course of a lifetime. Researchers hope to find ways to overcome such difficulties but it seems likely that the use of adult stem cells will take a long time to develop.

Researching a Cure

Insight into what happens in the brain when PD develops may lead to the development of effective new treatment approaches. For many diseases, such insights have come through the study of animal models—specially bred strains of laboratory animals that develop some or all of the typical symptoms of the human form of the disease. Now researchers have two handy animal models for the study of Parkinson's disease. Some human PD patients have been found to have a faulty gene for the protein alpha-synuclein. Copies of this mutant gene have been transferred to mice and fruit flies. Like the patients with the inherited form of PD, these experimental animals suffer damage

Drink Up!

For years, scientists have warned against drinking too much coffee, a product that can make people jittery. But a study reported in the *Journal of the American Medical Association* in May, 2000 suggested that coffee may possibly prevent Parkinson's disease. The study, led by Dr. G. Webster Ross, a neurologist at the Veterans Affairs Medical Center in Honolulu, included 8,004 Japanese-American male subjects in Hawaii who participated in a long-term study of possible causes of heart disease.

At the start of study, which began in 1965, the middle-aged participants ranged in age from forty-five to sixty-eight, with an average age of fifty-three. The subjects were asked about their coffee consumption when they enrolled in the study, and again six years later. Over a period of thirty years from the beginning of the study, 102 of the subjects developed Parkinson's disease. Men who were not coffee drinkers were two to three times more likely to develop PD than those who drank from four ounces to four six-ounce cups of coffee a day. The difference was even greater—five times more likely—when non-coffee drinkers were compared with men who drank a lot of coffee—four and a half to five and a half six-ounce cups a day.

The study suggested that caffeine was the key because similar results were found in people who ate foods containing caffeine. Dr. Ross theorized that caffeine might somehow protect heavy coffee drinkers against the cell destruction that causes Parkinson's disease. However, he contends that it is too early to recommend coffee as a treatment for Parkinson's, and it is unclear whether the same results would also apply to women, or to other ethnic groups. More research needs to be done on the possible benefits of caffeine and its effects on various parts of the brain.[24]

to dopamine-producing neurons in the brain and develop movement difficulties. The Parkinson-like disorders in the mice and fruit flies develop with advancing age, just as they do in human patients, and their brain cells also contain structures similar to the Lewy bodies characteristic of PD. Researchers are studying the animal models to determine whether they show the changes in energy metabolism and increase in oxidative stress typical of human PD patients. They also plan to produce fruit flies and mice with mutations in other key genes that have been found in patients with hereditary forms of PD, in order to obtain an animal model with all the characteristics of the human disease.[25]

In 2000, an international team of scientists announced that they had used gene therapy to deliver a protein called GDNF to the brains of experimental monkeys with Parkinson's disease. Earlier studies had shown that GDNF, a normal brain protein, could prevent the loss of dopamine-secreting neurons. The gene for the protein was spliced into a modified form of HIV, the AIDS virus, which had been stripped of its ability to cause disease. The genetically engineered virus was used to carry the gene past the blood-brain barrier and into the areas of the brain where it was needed. The treated monkeys had much better control of their muscle movements, and brain scans showed that their loss of dopamine neurons had stopped.[26]

With approaches such as these, researchers hope not only to develop better ways of controlling PD symptoms, but ultimately to cure the disease.

Q & A

Q. I've noticed that my grandmother seems awfully fidgety lately. Sometimes her finger twitches or she taps her foot when she's just sitting and watching TV. Is something wrong with her?

A. Maybe she is bored or worried about something. But it may be a good idea for her to see a doctor and get a checkup. What you describe could be early signs of Parkinson's disease or some other neurological problem.

Q. I thought Parkinson's disease was something only old people get, but now I hear that Michael J. Fox has it. Isn't he just a kid?

A. Actually, Michael J. Fox is older than he looks, but he has had the condition since he was about thirty. That is younger than the age when most people with Parkinson's first notice symptoms, but about 10 percent of PD cases start before the age of fifty.

Q. What is Parkinson's disease, anyway?

A. It is a condition in which the person's brain loses some of its ability to control movements; so the person may have tremors (shaking), muscle stiffness, poor balance, and slowness of movements.

Q. You mean the person is brain damaged? Like from a motorcycle accident?

A. Doctors are still not sure exactly what causes the destruction of cells in key areas of the brain involved in controlling and coordinating movements. In most cases, there has not been anything obvious like a head injury. In a small number of cases, it appears to be a hereditary condition, and scientists have isolated some of the genes involved.

Q. If you get Parkinson's disease, do you get over it after a while, like the flu?

A. Unfortunately, Parkinson's disease tends to get worse, not better, with time. And there is no shot or pill you can take to cure it. But there are drugs and other treatments that can ease the symptoms and slow down their progression to more severe problems. Researchers hope that new treatments being developed, such as transplants of healthy new brain cells grown in laboratory cultures, can bring Parkinson's patients back to normal and keep them that way.

Q. My uncle was taking medications for Parkinson's and started seeing things—like people and animals in his bedroom at night. Was it the drugs? The doctor put him on a different drug, and he was okay.

A. Sinemet and other drugs for PD may cause hallucinations in some people, especially older patients. Usually, reducing the dose of the drug or switching to a different combination of drugs can solve the problem.[1]

Q. I read that Michael J. Fox had surgery and they actually destroyed part of his brain to help with his Parkinson's symptoms. Isn't that dangerous?

A. There is a risk in any kind of surgery, but doctors have developed very precise techniques for locating and reaching the problem areas in the brain without damaging important structures.

Q. My Dad says he gets a sort of crawly feeling in his legs at night, and he twitches and thrashes and gets the covers all tangled up. But he has no problems during the daytime. Is he getting Parkinson's disease?

A. It sounds like he may have a condition called restless leg syndrome. It is not Parkinson's disease, but drugs used for PD can help to control it.[2]

Parkinson's Disease Timeline

2500 B.C.—Ancient evidence of Parkinson's included in Sanskrit texts.

1350 B.C.—An Egyptian papyrus describes Parkinson's symptoms.

100s A.D.—Greek physician Galen of Pergamum distinguishes between tremors that occur at rest and those that occur during movement.

late 1400s—Italian artist Leonardo da Vinci writes "Human beings who tremble without permission of the soul," which some historians believe could have been a description of PD.

1600s—German physician Franz de la Boë describes two kinds of tremors: during an activity and while the body is at rest.

1663—Dutch artist Rembrandt depicts Parkinson's disease in his famous etching, "The Good Samaritan."

mid-1700s—German physician Johann Juncker distinguishes between active and passive tremors.

late 1700s—German poet Johann Wolfgang von Goethe notes that the innkeeper in Rembrandt's etching appears to have tremors in his hands.

1817—James Parkinson is the first to describe the Parkinson's disease condition in his work, "An Essay on the Shaking Palsy."

1861—Jean-Martin Charcot and colleagues writes a series of articles on Parkinson's disease, which increases public awareness of PD.

1876—Jean-Martin Charcot changes "shaking palsy" to "Parkinson's disease" in honor of James Parkinson.

1895—Édouard Brissaud suggests that Parkinson's is due to damage in the substantial nigra.

1912—Frederick H. Lewy observes abnormal structures ("Lewy bodies") in some brain cells in autopsies on Parkinson's patients.

1919—C. Tretiakoff finds damaged cells in the substantial nigra of PD patients.

1938—German pathologist Rolf Hassler confirms Tretiakoff's findings.

1939—Russell Myers discoveries that brain surgery that removes key cells will ease PD symptoms.

1947—Henry Wycis and Ernst Spiegel builds a stereotactic setup for brain surgery using X-ray films to locate the nerve cluster precisely.

1960—Oleh Hornykiewicz and Walter Birkmayer first treat Parkinson's patients with L-dopa to replace the missing dopamine. Symptoms improves, but severe side effects resulted due to high dosage.

1966—George Cotzias discover that gradual increases in the L-dopa dose ease symptoms and reduce side effects.

1970—The Food and Drug Administration (FDA) approves levodopa for standard treatment of Parkinson's disease.

1988—Curt Freed performs the first fetal-cell transplant for PD.

1989—DA approves deprenyl for the treatment of PD.

1995—Studies of xenotransplants of fetal-pig brain cells in human PD patients begin.

1999—Researchers isolate stem cells from adults and demonstrate that they can be transformed into specialized cells for different kinds of tissues.

For More Information

American Parkinson's
Disease Association
1250 Hylan Boulevard
Staten Island, NY 10305
1(800) 223-APDA
<http://www.apdaparkinson.com>

National Institute of Neurological
Disorders and Stroke
Office of Communications and
Public Liaison
P.O. Box 5801
Bethesda, MD 20824
1(800) 352-9424
<http://www.ninds.nih.gov>

National Parkinson's Foundation, Inc.
1501 N.W. 9th Avenue (Bob Hope Road)
Miami, FL 33136-1494
1(800) 327-4545
<http://www.parkinson.org>

Parkinson's Action Network
840 Third Street
Santa Rosa, CA 95404
1(800) 850-4726
<http://info@parkinsonaction.org>

Parkinson's Disease
Foundation, Inc.
William Black Medical
Research Building
Columbia-Presbyterian
Medical Center
710 West 168th Street
New York, NY 10032
1(800) 457-6676
<http://www.pdf.org>

Parkinson's Institute
1170 Morse Avenue
Sunnyvale, CA 94089-1605
1(800) 786-2958
<http://www.parkinsonsinstitute.org/>

United Parkinson's Foundation
833 W. Washington Boulevard
Chicago, IL 60607
(312) 733-1893

World Parkinson's Disease Association
via Zuretti, 35
20125 Milano, Italy
E-mail: info@aolwpda.org
<http://www.wpda.org/>

Chapter Notes

Chapter 1. The Shaking Disease

1. MovieThing.com, "Michael J. Fox: A Biography." <http://moviething.com/bios/michaeljfox> (March 30, 2000).

2. Karen S. Schneider and Todd Gold, "After the Tears," *People Magazine*, December 7, 1998, p. 129.

3. Ibid., p. 128.

4. Ibid., p. 130.

5. "Michael J. Fox leaving 'Spin City,'" *The Times of India*, January 20, 2000, <http://www.timesofindia.com/200100/ 20more1.htm> (April 4, 2000).

6. The Associated Press, "Fox pushes Senate for funds," *The Courier News* (Bridgewater, NJ), September 29, 1999, p. A-7.

7. "A Graceful Good-bye," *TV Guide*, May 13, 2000, pp. 22–28, 78.

8. Ibid., p. 74.

Chapter 2. The History of Parkinson's Disease

1. Sue Dauphin, *Parkinson's Disease: the Mystery, the Search, and the Promise* (Tequesta, FL: Pixel Press, 1992), pp. 20-22; James Parkinson, *An Essay on the Shaking Palsy* (London: Whittingham and Rowland, 1817), pp. 1–18.

2. Jan Keppel Hesselink, "History of PD," January 6, 1997, <http://dem0nmac.mgh.harvard.edu/neurowebforum/ParkinsonsDisease Articles/1.6.977.30AMHistoryofPD.html>

3. Sue Dauphin, p. 22.

4. Abraham N. Lieberman and Frank L. Williams, *Parkinson's Disease: the Complete Guide for Patients and Caregivers* (New York: Simon and Schuster, 1993), p. 25; Roger C. Duvoisin and Jacob Sage, *Parkinson's Disease: A Guide for Patient and Family* (Philadelphia, PA: Lippincott-Raven Publishers, 1996), p. 128; Sue Dauphin, pp. 29–30.

5. Abraham N. Lieberman and Frank L. Williams, p. 25; Sue Dauphin, p. 30.

6. Sue Dauphin, pp. 29-30; Roger C. Duvoisin and Jacob Sage, p. 128.

7. Abraham N. Lieberman and Frank L. Williams, p. 25; James Parkinson, p. 172; *Encyclopaedia Britannica.* (Chicago: Encyclopaedia Britannica, 1973), Vol. 21, p. 557.

8. Sue Dauphin, pp. 23-24; James Parkinson, pp. 20–21.

9. Sue Dauphin, p. 25.

10. Jan Keppel Hesselink.

11. Abraham N. Lieberman and Frank L. Williams, p. 31.

12. Sue Dauphin, pp. 30–31.

13. Ibid., pp. 55–56.

14. Ibid., p. 35.

15. Ibid., p. 32.

16. Ibid., pp. 69–83.

17. Ibid., pp. 42–54.

Chapter 3. What is Parkinson's Disease?

1. "U.S. Dept. of Justice: Office of the Attorney General—Janet Reno's Bio," <http://www.usdoj.gov/ag/jreno.html> (April 12, 2000).

2. Pierre Thomas and David Brown, "Attorney General Janet Reno Diagnosed With Parkinson's," *The Washington Post*, November 17, 1995, p. 2, <http://www-tech.mit.edu/V115/N57/reno.57w.html>.

3. Carol Rosenberg, "Disease Has Not Halted Reno," *The Miami Herald*, <http://www.parkinson.org/herald/reno.htm> (April 12, 2000).

4. Sheryl Gay Stolberg, "Reno Puts a Public Face on an Often Private Disease," *The New York Times*, August 15, 1999, p. 16.

5. Carol Rosenberg.

6. Sheryl Gay Stolberg.

7. Pierre Thomas and David Brown, "Attorney General Janet Reno Diagnosed With Parkinson's," *The Washington Post*, November 17, 1995, <http://www-tech.mit.edu/V115/N57/reno.57w.html>.

8. John Henkel, "Parkinson's Disease: New Treatments Slow Onslaught of Symptoms," Northwest Parkinson's Foundation, <http://www.nwpf.org/news/item991228/item991228a.html> (April 12, 2000).

9. The National Parkinson's Foundation, Inc., "What the Patient Should Know." <http://www.parkinson.org:80/pdedu.htm> (March 21, 2000).

10. John Henkel.

11. Abraham N. Lieberman and Frank L. Williams. *Parkinson's Disease: the Complete Guide for Patients and Caregivers* (New York: Simon and Schuster, 1993), p. 21.

12. Abraham N. Lieberman and Frank L. Williams, pp. 28-35.

13. Arthur C. Guyton and John E. Hall, *Textbook of Medical Physiology*, 9th Edition (Philadelphia, PA: W.B. Saunders, 1996), pp. 715–731.

14. The American Parkinson's Disease Association, Inc. *Parkinson's Disease Handbook: A Guide for Patients and Their Families*, 1996, p. 20.

15. Roger C. Duvoisin and Jacob Sage. Parkinson's Disease: *A Guide for Patient and Family* (Philadelphia, PA: Lippincott-Raven Publishers, 1996), pp. 138–139; The American Parkinson's Disease Association, Inc., p. 20.

16. The American Parkinson's Disease Association, Inc., p. 20.

17. David L. Cram. *Understanding Parkinson's Disease* (Omaha, NE: Addicus Books, Inc., 1999), pp. 5-8; The American Parkinson's Disease Association, Inc., pp. 3-5; National Institute of Neurological Disorders and Stroke, "Parkinson's disease: Hope Through Research," <http://www.ninds.nih.gov/health_and_medical/pubs/parkinson_disease_htr.htm> (March 21, 2000); Abraham N. Lieberman and Frank L. Williams, pp. 13–20.

18. David L. Cram, pp. 10–11.

Chapter 4. What Causes Parkinson's Disease?

1. Abraham N. Lieberman and Frank L. Williams. *Parkinson's Disease: the Complete Guide for Patients and Caregivers* (New York: Simon and Schuster, 1993), pp. 27-28; Elaine Landau. *Parkinson's Disease* (New York: Franklin Watts, 1999), pp. 28-29; Roger C. Duvoisin and Jacob Sage, *Parkinson's Disease: A Guide for Patient and Family* (Philadelphia, PA: Lippincott-Raven Publishers, 1996), p. 132.

2. Elaine Landau, pp. 28-29; Biography (Oliver Sacks), <http://www.oliversacks.com/bio.html> (April 21, 2000); "Awakenings (Republished Sept. 99 by Vintage Books)." <http://www.oliversacks.com/awakenings.html> (April 21, 2000).

3. Abraham N. Lieberman and Frank L. Williams, pp. 41–42; Elaine Landau, pp. 29-30.

4. Moussa B. H. Youdim and Peter Riederer, "Understanding Parkinson's Disease," *Scientific American,* January 1997, p. 52.

5. The American Parkinson's Disease Association, Inc. *Parkinson's Disease Handbook: A Guide for Patients and Their Families,* 1996, pp. 2.

6. William Plummer, "The World's Champion," *People Magazine,* January 13, 1997, p. 46.

7. The American Parkinson's Disease Association, *Young Parkinson's Handbook,* 1995, p. 5.

8. Roger C. Duvoisin and Jacob Sage, *Parkinson's Disease: A Guide for Patient and Family* (Philadelphia, PA: Lippincott-Raven Publishers, 1996), p. 147; Robert Hauser and Theresa Zesiewicz. *Parkinson's Disease: Questions and Answers* (Coral Springs, FL: Merit Publishing International, 1999), p. 45.

9. Division of Intramural Research: Background information: Parkinson's disease, p. 2, <http://www.nhgri.nih.gov/DIR/LGDR/PARK/about_parks.html> (March 21, 2000); David Nicholl, "Familial Parkinson's disease—Frequently asked questions," p. 3, <http://medweb.bham.ac.uk/clin_neuro/genetics/faq.html> (April 11, 2000); Parkinson's Research Group, Mayo Clinic Jacksonville, "Parkinson's Disease: Genetic advances," <http://www.mayo.edu/fpd/hugo.htm> (April 25, 2000); Parkinson's Disease Foundation Newsletter, "A Parkinson's Gene is Discovered," October 1997, p. 2.

10. Roger C. Duvoisin and Jacob Sage, pp. 147–148.

11. Parkinson's Research Group, Mayo Clinic Jacksonville.

12. David Nicholl.

13. Roger C. Duvoisin and Jacob Sage, pp. 135–138; Abraham N. Lieberman and Frank L. Williams, pp. 42–43, 46.

14. P. F. Good, C. W. Olanow, and D. P. Perl. "Neuromelanin-containing neurons of the substantial nigra accumulate iron and aluminum in Parkinson's disease: a LAMMA study," *Brain Research*, October, 16, 1992, pp. 343-346; M. Yasui, T. Kihira, and K. Ota, "Calcium, magnesium and aluminum concentrations in Parkinson's disease," *Neurotoxicology*, Fall 1992, pp. 593-600; D. P. Perl and P. F. Good, "Aluminum and the neurofibrillary tangle: results of tissue microprobe studies," *Ciba Foundation Symposium*, 1992, pp. 217–227.

15. Roger C. Duvoisin and Jacob Sage, pp. 135-138; Abraham N. Lieberman and Frank L. Williams, pp. 42–43, 46.

16. Sandra Blakeslee, "Pesticide Found to Produce Parkinson's Symptoms in Rats," *The New York Times*, November 5, 2000, p. 38.

17. P. F. Good, C. W. Olanow, and D. P. Perl; pp. 343-346; M. Yasui, T. Kihira, and K. Ota, pp. 593-600; D. P. Perl and P. F. Good, pp. 217–227.

18. Robert Hauser and Theresa Zesiewicz, pp. 46-52.

19. Hans R. Larsen, "Parkinson's Disease: Is Victory in Sight?" *International Journal of Alternative and Complementary Medicine,* October 1997, pp. 22–24; <http://vvv.com/HealthNews/dparrewb.html>.

20. Ibid.

Chapter 5. Diagnosing Parkinson's Disease

1. Abraham N. Lieberman and Frank L. Williams. *Parkinson's Disease: the Complete Guide for Patients and Caregivers* (New York: Simon and Schuster, 1993), pp. 7–8.

2. Ibid.

3. Mayo Clinic Health Oasis, "Essential Tremor: Getting a better grasp on this bothersome condition," 2000, <http://www.mayohealth. org/mayo/9701/htm/essentia.htm> (May 3, 2000); Abraham N. Lieberman and Frank L. Williams, p. 253; The Parkinson's Institute, "Essential Tremor," <http://www.parkinsoninstitute.org/tremor.html> (May 3, 2000).

4. Elaine Landau. *Parkinson's Disease* (New York: Franklin Watts, 1999), pp. 32–33.

5. Abraham N. Lieberman and Frank L. Williams, pp. 8–10.

6. Ibid., pp. 10–11.

7. Anne Eisenberg, "An Early Warning for Parkinson's," *The New York Times*, June 25, 2000, p. WH 3.

Chapter 6. Treating Parkinson's Disease

1. Earl Ubell, "Trembling, With Hope," *Parade Magazine*, October 10, 1993, p. 16.

2. Gina Kolata, "Parkinson's Sufferers Gamble On Surgery With Great Risks," *The New York Times*, March 16, 1995, pp. A1, B11.

3. David L. Cram. *Understanding Parkinson's Disease* (Omaha, NE: Addicus Books, Inc., 1999), pp. 50-54; Elaine Landau. *Parkinson's Disease* (New York: Franklin Watts, 1999), pp. 40–44.

4. Laura Spinney, "Seeing is Unfreezing," *New Scientist*, February 15, 1997, pp. 38-40.

5. David L. Cram, pp. 50–54; Elaine Landau, pp. 40–44.

6. The American Parkinson's Disease Association, *Young Parkinson's Handbook*, 1995, p. 16.

7. P. A. Kempster and M. L. Wahlqvist, "Dietary factors in the management of Parkinson's disease," *Nutrition Reviews*, February 1994, pp. 51–58.

8. The American Parkinson's Disease Association, p. 18; David L. Cram, pp. 57–60.

9. Nathan Seppa, "An Alternate Approach to Parkinson's," *Science News*, June 10, 2000, p. 381.

10. Elena Portyansky, "Promising Research Brings Hope to Parkinson's Patients," *Drug Topics*, October 18, 1999, p. 40.

11. "Surgery Relieves Parkinson's Symptoms in Some Patients," Medical College of Georgia, March 1999, <http://www.mcg.edu/news/96newsrel/pallidotomy.html>; "Parkinson's Disease," WebMD/Lycos, <http://webmd.lycos.com/content/dmk/dmk_article_ 40066> (March 21, 2000); David L. Cram, pp. 69–71.

12 David L. Cram, pp. 71–72.

13. Ibid., pp. 70–72.

14. Ibid., pp. 72–73; "Parkinson's Disease," WebMD/Lycos.

15. Abraham N. Lieberman and Frank L. Williams. *Parkinson's Disease: the Complete Guide for Patients and Caregivers* (New York: Simon and Schuster, 1993), p. 83.

16. Paul G. Donohue, "High-protein diets affect some Parkinson's patients," *The Star-Ledger* (Newark, NJ), May 23, 1989, p. 32.

17. Abraham N. Lieberman and Frank L. Williams, pp. 77–78.

18. Julie McDowell, "Therapy with rhythm," *Modern Drug Discovery*, May 2000, p.

19. National Institute of Neurological Disorders and Stroke, "Parkinson's Disease: Hope Through Research," <http://www.ninds.nih.gov /patients/Disorder/parkinso/pdhtr.htm> (March 21, 2000).

Chapter 7. Parkinson's Disease and Society

1. Joe Territo, "A Leg Up on Parkinson's: Walkers raise funds for drug research," *The Star-Ledger* (Newark, NJ), July 28, 1991, p. 13.

2. Karen S. Schneider and Todd Gold, "After the Tears," *People Magazine*, 12/7/98, pp. 126–136.

3. Geoffrey Cowley, "The New War on Parkinson's," *Newsweek*, May 22, 2000, pp. 52–58.

4. "Reno: 'I am running for governor'," CNN, September 5, 2001, <http://www.cnn.com/2001/ALLPOLITICS/09/04/reno.governor>.

5. AP, "Fla. Governor Bid by Reno Likely," *The Courier-News* (Bridgewater, NJ), September 4, 2001, p. A-8.

6. Rhonda Rowland, "Dog proves to be best friend for Parkinson's sufferer," *CNN Interactive*, December 29, 1997, <http://www.cnn.com/HEALTH/9712/29/parkinsons.dogs/index.html>.

7. Larry Muhammad, "A good relationship," *The Courier News* (Bridgewater, NJ), September 19, 1999, p. C-5.

8. Guy Sterling and Stephen Steele, "Should boxing be banned? *The Star-Ledger* (Newark, NJ), December 4, 1994, p. 1–2, sec. 6.

9. Susan Imke, Trudy Hutton, and Sheree Loftus, "Parkinson's Disease: Caring and Coping," The National Parkinson's Foundation, Inc., 1996-2001, <http://www.parkinson.org:80/care5.htm>.

10. Ibid., "How Do We Define Caregiving? NFCA Member Survey 1997" <http://www.parkinson.org:80/care12.htm>.

Chapter 8. Parkinson's Disease and the Future

1. Sheryl Gay Stolberg, "Decisive Moment on Parkinson's Fetal-Cell Transplants," *The New York Times*, April 20, 1999, p. F-2.

2. Ibid.

3. Geoffrey Cowley, "The New War on Parkinson's," *Newsweek,* May 22, 2000, p. 57; Parkinson's Disease Foundation, "First Controlled Test of Brain Cell Transplants Yields Mixed Results," *The PDF News* (quarterly publication), Spring/Summer 1999, p. 1, 8.

4. Sheryl Gay Stolberg.

5. Ibid.

6. "The Many Uses of Fetal Tissue," <http://members.aol.com/poesgirl/fetal.html> (May 23, 2000); Planned Parenthood, "Donating Fetal Tissue for Medical Treatment and Research," <http://www.plannedparenthood.org/library/facts/fetaltis_010600.html> (April 28, 2000).

7. Sheryl Gay Stolberg.

8. Elaine Landau. *Parkinson's Disease* (New York: Franklin Watts, 1999), p. 64.

9. Sheryl Gay Stolberg.

10. Ibid.

11. Geoffrey Cowley, pp. 56–57.

12. Ibid.

13. N. Seppa, "Pig-cell grafts ease symptoms of Parkinson's," *Science News*, March 25, 2000, p. 197.

14. A.J. Hostetler, "First piglets cloned from adult sow's cells/Organ transplant applications cited," *Times-Dispatch*, March 15, 2000, <http://www.timesdispatch.com/health/pigs15.shtml>.

15. Paul Candon, "Parkinson's Patients Improve With Pig-Cell Transplants 3/14," *Medical Tribune*, March 14, 2000, <http://www. 199.97.97.16/IMDS%7CWeek%7C/home/content/users/imds/nytsyn/20 00/03/15/medic/7465-0010-pat_nytimes%7C%C>; Cheryl Grogan, "Pig tissue transplant may improve Parkinson's disease," The American Academy of Neurology release, March 13, 2000, <http://www. eurekalert.org/releases/aane-ptt030700.html>; Dan Vergano, "Pig cells a safe option for Parkinson's," *USA Today*, March 14, 2000, <http://www. usatoday.com/life/health/brain/lhbra053.htm>.

16. N. Seppa; A. J. Hostetler.

17. N. Seppa; Paul Candon; Cheryl Grogan.

18. Xiao-Zhong Liu, John W. McDonald, et al., "Transplanted embryonic stem cells survive, differentiate and promote recovery in injured rat spinal cord," *Nature Medicine*, December 1999, pp. 1410–1412.

19. Christine Gorman, "Brave New Cells," *Newsweek,* May 1, 2000, pp. 58–60.

20. Geoffrey Cowley, pp. 56-57; Natalie Larsen, "Cultured Neural Stem Cells Reduce Symptoms in Model of Parkinson's Disease," National Institutes of Health, <http://www.nih.gov/news/pr/july98/ninds-20.htm> (May 30, 2000).

21. Associated Press, "'Superman' actor lobbies Congress for embryo research," *The Dallas Morning News*, April 27, 2000, <http://www .dallasnews.com/national/70311_CELLS27.html>.

22. Frank Bruni and Katharine Q. Seelye, "Bush Gives His Backing for Limited Research on Existing Stem Cells," *The New York Times*, August 10, 2001, pp. A1, A16, A17.

23. Christine Gorman.

24. Ibid.; National Institutes of Health, "Stem Cells: A Primer," May 2000, <http://www.nih.gov/news/stemcell/primer.htm>.

25. Valina L. Dawson, "Of Flies and Mice," *Science*, April 28, 2000, pp. 631–632.

26. Lindsey Tanner, "Caffeine May Deter Parkinson's," Associated Press, May 24, 2000, <http://www.ap.org/APnews/center_story.html?FRONTID=SCIENCE&STORYID=APIS74LS43O0>; G. Webster Ross et al., "Association of Coffee and Caffeine Intake with the Risk of Parkinson's Disease," *Journal of the American Medical Association*, May 24/31, 2000, pp. 2674–2679.

27. Jeffrey H. Kordower, Marina E. Emborg, et al., "Neurodegeneration Prevented by Lentiviral Vector Delivery of GDNF in Primate Models of Parkinson's Disease," *Science*, October 27, 2000, pp. 767–773; Lars Olsen, "Combatting Parkinson's Disease: Step Three," Ibid., pp. 721–724.

Q & A

1. William Reichman, "Medication for Parkinson's Can Cause Hallucinations," *The Star-Ledger* (Newark, NJ), July 11, 2000, p. 26.

2. Paul G. Donohue, "Be Still, My Restless Legs," *The Star-Ledger* (Newark, NJ), July 3, 2000, p. 32.

Glossary

anesthetic—A drug used to reduce sensitivity to pain or to produce unconsciousness during surgery.

anticholinergic drugs—Medication used to block the action of the neurotransmitter acetocholine.

antioxidants—Substances that protect body chemicals from oxidative reactions and the potentially harmful free radicals they generate.

axon—A single, long, hair-like fiber that extends from the cell body, by which it sends messages from one nerve cell to another.

basal ganglia—Several large clusters of nerve cells deep in the brain that coordinate motor control; includes striatum and substantial nigra.

blood-brain barrier—A complicated network of tiny blood vessels and cells that screens out many chemicals in the blood and protects the delicate brain cells from their possibly harmful effects.

bradykinesia—Slowness of movement.

central nervous system (CNS)—The brain and spinal cord.

cerebellum—A part of the brain that that monitors body parts and coordinates movements.

cerebral cortex—The thin, outermost layer of the brain where most of the activity in the brain takes place.

cerebrum—The largest part of the brain, with which we think, remember, make decisions, and control the movements of the body.

COMT—Catechol-O-methyltransferase, an enzyme that converts levodopa to an inactive product.

corpus striatum—An area in the basal ganglia, which controls movement, balance, and walking.

cryosurgery—The use of extreme cold to destroy tissue for medical purposes.

deep brain stimulation (DBS)—A procedure in which a high-frequency electric current is used to paralyze overactive brain cells.

122

dendrite—Thread-like fibers extending from the neuron, which receive messages from other nerve cells.

dopamine—A chemical substance (neurotransmitter) found in the part of the brain that controls movement, balance, and walking.

dopamine agonists—Drugs that work by stimulating dopamine receptors in the basal ganglia, thus mimicking the effects of dopamine.

dyskinesia—Involuntary and uncontrollable movements that occur in many Parkinson's patients who are treated with levodopa. These movements may include nodding, jerking, and twitching.

electrode—A device that picks up electric currents.

electroencephalogram (EEG)—A device that records electric currents generated by the brain.

encephalitis—Also called sleeping sickness; inflammation of the brain.

enzyme—A protein that helps chemical reactions to proceed, without being changed itself in the process.

essential tremor—Progressive, neurological disorder, which may occur in the elderly or the young and gradually worsen over time; this condition resembles Parkinson's because tremors are a hallmark of the disease.

festination—Taking quick steps to keep a person's balance.

free radicals—Highly reactive chemical particles produced by oxidation.

globus pallidus—A structure in the basal ganglia that contains nerve cells that transmit messages for movement.

idiopathic Parkinson's disease—Parkinson's cases that have no known cause.

limbic system—A group of structures in the brain involved in emotional feelings and reactions.

magnetic resonance imaging (MRI)—A process of producing images of the body using radio waves and a magnetic field.

mitochondria—Specialized structures inside body cells which contain their own genetic information and produce energy by oxidative reactions.

monoamine oxidase (MAO B)—An enzyme in the brain that breaks down dopamine.

MPTP—A chemical by-product from making a synthetic narcotic; MPTP kills the cells in the substantial nigra and produces Parkinson's-like symptoms.

neurons—Nerve cells.

neurotransmitters—Chemicals that help in carrying messages from one nerve cell to another.

oxidation—A process that uses oxygen to release energy.

pallidotomy—A surgical procedure in which key nerve cells are removed from the globus pallidus, located in the basal ganglia.

parkinsonism—A name used to describe conditions that exhibit Parkinson's-like symptoms including tremors, stiffness, slowness of movement.

positron emission tomography—Also called PET scan; an imaging technique using radioactive particles called positrons to "tag" glucose and show which brain cells are active.

postencephalitic parkinsonism—A Parkinson's-like condition that developed after a particular kind of encephalitis.

primary parkinsonism—Also known as idiopathic Parkinson's disease.

pugilistic parkinsonism—A Parkinson's-like condition that occurs in boxers who receive multiple blows to the head.

rigidity—Stiffness.

secondary parkinsonism—Parkinson's-like conditions that do have a known cause, such as drug-induced, viral, or head trauma.

shaking palsy—Also called paralysis agitans; the name that was once used to describe what is now commonly known as Parkinson's disease.

stem cells—Primitive cells that have the potential to develop into any cells or tissues in the body.

stereotactic surgery—A technique that uses X-ray films to precisely locate the intended target area.

substantial nigra—A cluster of black-pigmented nerve cells found in a tiny area deep within the brain.

synapse—A fluid-filled gap that separates the axon terminal from the dendrite of the neighboring neuron. Neurotransmitters travel through the synapse, carrying messages from one nerve cell to another.

syndrome—A group of symptoms that generally occur together in a particular disease.

thalamus—A central relay station in the brain that transmits sensory messages.

thalamotomy—A surgical procedure in which key nerve cells are removed from the thalamus, a message relay station in the midbrain.

tremor—An involuntary trembling, shaking, or quivering.

xenotransplantation—Transplanting cells from other species.

young-onset Parkinson's—Development of PD symptoms in people under fifty.

Further Reading

Books

Cram, David L. *Understanding Parkinson's Disease.* Omaha, Nebraska: Addicus Books, Inc., 1999.

Landau, Elaine. *Parkinson's Disease.* New York: Franklin Watts, 1999.

McGoon, Dwight C. *The Parkinson's Handbook.* New York: W.W. Norton and Company, 1990.

Internet Addresses

HealthAtoZ.com: "What is Parkinson's Disease?"

<http://www.healthatoz.com/healthatoz/Atoz/dc/caz/neur/park/parkwhat.html>

Michael J. Fox Foundation for Parkinson's Research

<http://michaeljfox.org>

ParkinsonsInfo.com: Frequently Asked Questions

<http://www.parkinsonsinfo.com/faq>

Index

N

nerve cells
  degeneration, 11
  effects of surgical procedures, 24, 25, 26, 77, 78
  identification for scan, 68
  identification for surgery, 25–26, 110
  normal, 18, 32–33, 34, 35
  regeneration, 94, 99–104, 110
neurotransmitters, 11, 20, 34, 35. *See also* Dopamine; Levodopa

P

parkinsonism
  postencephalitic, 45–46
  pugilistic, 49
  secondary, 44
  vs. Parkinson's disease, 11, 38
patient history, 64
pesticides and herbicides, 56–57
physical examination, 64–66
positron emission tomography (PET), 67, 67–68, 81
progression of symptoms, 43, 59, 74, 80, 108
public awareness, 9, 10, 30, 32, 83–85

R

Reno, Janet, 27–30, 28, 85
research
  current, 9, 10, 50–52, 54–56, 91–106, 110
  early, 13–16, 17–26, 109–110
  funding and ethical issues, 95, 101
resources for information, 111, 126

S

skin problems, 42
sleep problems, 42
speech problems, 5, 42
stem-cell research, 94, 99–104, 110
stiffness, *See* Muscle rigidity

substantia nigra, 18–20, 21, 22, 36–37, 55, 58, 109, 110
swallowing and chewing difficulties, 5, 42, 84
symptoms
  in early writings, 14–15, 16, 17, 109
  monitoring, for diagnosis, 64
  summary, 5, 39–44

T

target population, 5, 30–32, 61
timeline, 109–110
treatment, 69–82. *See also* Brain surgery; Drug therapy
tremors
  active, 16, 17, 62
  cause, 37
  effects of deep brain stimulation, 79
  essential, 62
  at rest, 5, 16, 17, 39–40, 62
  role in diagnosis, 64–66

U

urinary problems, 42
U.S. Congress, 9, 10

V

virtual reality device, 73
vitamins, 59, 80

W

walking
  brain function during, 36
  difficulty in, 14, 15, 17, 18, 20, 40, 41
  during physical exam, 65
  "tricks" to help, 74
young patients, 31

X

xenotransplants, 96–99, 99, 110

Y

young-onset Parkinson's, 5, 30, 31, 107